Contents

Introduction		**2**
Matthew 5–7	The successful life	**7**
Leviticus 1–25	When God moves in…	**22**
1 Corinthians 8–10	Living for God and others	**30**
Matthew 8–10	What kind of man is this?	**39**
2 Samuel	Being his	**59**
Acts 20–23	Solemnly testifying	**67**
Matthew 11,12	Surprise, surprise!	**82**
2 Samuel	Being his *continued*	**90**
Matthew 26–28	God longs to be with us	**98**
Feature		
SU article	Sam's gift	**4**
Spotlight on…	The love of God	**55**
Bible in a year	Pull-out and keep	**56**

A new year, a new you?

Maybe every year you intend to be more consistent with your *Daily Bread* readings? Maybe you never miss a day? Or maybe this is the first time you've ever picked up a copy? Whoever you are, I want to challenge you this New Year to go deeper. For years *Daily Bread* notes have included at the bottom of each page a 'Bible in a year' plan for readers to follow. This year we want to encourage more to do this, so a pull-out plan to keep track of your reading is available in the centre of this issue. Pull it out, keep it in each quarter's copy of *Daily Bread*, and after you've focused in on the main reading and note, go deeper by reading the whole Bible this year. Of course, in the early days, following a list of daily readings was more or less what it meant to be a part of 'the Children's Scripture Union'. For more inspiration, enjoy Ron Frost's introductory piece, 'Sam's gift', where he recounts his formative experience of meeting an older man who knew God and his Word so well, simply because he read it and read it.

New Year's resolutions often fail, and the reality is, that is because there is something deeply wrong with every one of us – we do not do what we want to do, but what we hate to do (Romans 7:15). Who can rescue us from these bodies of death?

Jesus can! So let's daily remember that there is no condemnation for those who are in Christ Jesus, and that his Spirit lives in us. And then each day come to his Word to be renewed and refreshed, guided by these excellent notes, and going deeper into God. And then let's go out as his hands and mouthpiece into a world in desperate need of him. That would be a good start to the new year.

Angus Moyes
Editor

How to use Daily Bread

Way in

This page introduces both the notes and the writer. It sets the scene and tells you what you need to know to get into each series.

A day's note

The notes for each day include five key elements: Prepare, Read (the Bible passage for the day), Explore, Respond and Bible in a year. These are intended to provide a helpful way of meeting God in his Word.

Prepare yourself to meet with God and pray that the Holy Spirit will help you to understand and respond to what you read.

Read the Bible passage, taking time to absorb and simply enjoy it. A verse or two from the Bible text is usually included on each page, but it's important to read the whole passage.

Explore the meaning of the passage, listening for what God may be saying to you. Before you read the comment, ask yourself: what's the main point of this passage? What is God showing me about himself or about my life? Is there a promise or a command, a warning or example to take special notice of?

Respond to what God has shown you in the passage in worship and pray for yourself and others. Decide how to share your discoveries with others.

Bible in a year If your aim is to know God and his Word more deeply, why not follow this plan to read the whole Bible in one year?

Sam's gift

I was 18 when I met Sam Cassel, a 70-year-old Scot and retired missionary. Retirement aside, Sam and his wife were planting a church in Sechelt, British Columbia. Two of us teens had been sent by our Spokane church to help construct a building for them.

Each morning Steve and I were invited to breakfast with the Cassels at their beachside cottage before work. Almost every morning – with just a little stir – Sam happily offered an impromptu survey of a biblical theme. At our first breakfast, for instance, I noticed the impressive trees near their house. He smiled and talked about the importance of trees in the Bible, beginning with Eden, then the tree theme in Galatians and, finally, the reappearance of the Tree of Life in Revelation. The next morning he picked up on something else I said and used it to review all the Bible references to Melchizedek. I was impressed and enriched.

His broad awareness of the Bible was always personal and practical, with a depth that had me reflecting on the conversation for hours afterwards. I finally asked him where it came from – thinking of a possible college course – and he laughed.

'I just read my Bible.'

He had been reading his Bible, front to back, for 30 minutes each day since he came to faith 50 years before. The result? Two or three 'read-throughs' each year – with the outcome of almost 150 readings in his Christian life. And it showed!

I pressed Sam for more of his story. When he and his bride were both newly converted in 1916, they wanted the Lord to be at the centre of their new marriage. So Bible reading was something they shared each day. Not necessarily by reading aloud together – though they did that at times – but by sharing some of their favourite verses of the day at dinnertime. It was a firm feature of their married life.

I'm realistic in telling this story. Sam and his wife were a rare sighting! But why not start on the path they offered? Just over ten minutes of reading a day will cover the Bible in a year. And, in ten years, it offers the potential wealth of ten Bible read-throughs! Or even 50 after 50 years. The benefits can't be measured!

Sam's story certainly stirred me. Within the week I started my own unguided read-through and finished in less than two months. I was surprised to find God's character jumping off the pages. His greatness, goodness, and love as the triune Father-Son-and-Spirit God stirs the heart. I experienced his presence as both captivating and relational as I read, and realised God is always pursuing me through my reading of his Word!

Recently I reached my own 50-year mark of following Sam's example. So now I'd like to pass on Sam's baton of annual – or more – Bible read-throughs to readers who will, in turn, pass the gift on to others.

And that brings me to a second part of my story: to the joy of reading with a partner.

At first my daily Bible reading was strictly private. Then, still in the days of America's compulsory national service, I found myself in the US Army stationed next to the Pentagon.

John, my army roommate, had a thin version of Christian faith. One morning before I went to work he spoke of being badgered about his faith by the men in our military police unit. 'They're always after me,' he complained, 'but they never bother you.'

'Johnny,' I pushed back with the tenderness of a drill sergeant, 'it's because you don't stand for anything! You say you believe in God, but you never seem to spend any time with him. If you claim to be a Christian, why don't you show it?'

I asked him about his Bible reading. Had he ever read the Bible through?

The exchange came over breakfast and I had to go to work; but John had the day off. I felt guilty for being sharp with him so at noon I headed back to our flat for lunch ready to offer a rehearsed apology. I started but he waved me off – 'No, I needed to hear it.'

Then he gushed, 'This is good!'

He was in the easy chair, Bible in hand, and almost halfway through

Genesis. By that evening he made it through most of Exodus! Soon he was carrying his Bible to work and at breaks he would read segments to his amazed military police friends. He finished reading the entire Bible in just six weeks!

John quickly gained new credibility with his friends and ended any badgering. He also became a strong presence in the church we attended. In the meantime we spontaneously started sharing verses aloud whenever we were at the apartment doing our separate reading. He was in one section of the Bible and I was in another, but it didn't matter. We just enjoyed swapping verses with each other whenever a verse struck a chord. We loved it!

After the army he went on to Bible college. Before he left we talked about our Bible sharing and he summed up the result: 'I came to love God through my reading.' That's what we were actually sharing: a common delight in hearing from the living God who loves us.

I've since used this partner-reading approach with dozens of men, with a little bit of added structure. Our approach follows the discipleship ideal of 2 Timothy 2:2 – where Paul called on Timothy to share with others what he learned from Paul. With that in mind I asked a friend to join me in a Bible read-through. He agreed to it and we were off and running.

Here's the outline. Each week we read separately and then meet up for an hour to swap some of our underlined verses from the week. We avoid loose paraphrases or mini-sermonettes by each reading our verses verbatim – it gives God a voice! One of us takes ten minutes to read, arbitrarily, as many underlined verses as possible. We then swap roles as reader and listener. Sometimes we overlap verses but it doesn't matter. The point is that we both hear how God is touching our hearts. Some sharing and prayer is always part of the visit.

I call this 'Sam's gift' – and I'm happy to share it with you as a pathway to get to know and enjoy God more than ever before. And please find a partner – you'll both love it!

Writer
Ron Frost

Way in to Matthew 5–7

The successful life

The New Year invites us to new beginnings – to improve ourselves. Jesus answers this urge in his Sermon on the Mount. All who want to live more successful lives are invited to sit at his feet with open hearts. But the invitation carries some surprises.

Jesus spoke to his disciples with the compassion of a shepherd caring for his sheep. He treated them as needy; as vulnerable to the daily challenges of life. They were the 'poor in spirit' and those 'who mourn'. He spoke to them as frail and weak; as the insulted, the persecuted, and the misjudged.

As disciples their common bond was a faith in Jesus and their biggest challenges were 'because of me' (5:11). Today we have our own challenges as disciples: the sermon still works.

The biggest surprise is that Jesus doesn't invite disciples to the ordinary paths of life. He startles us by repeating, 'You have heard … but I tell you!' Old childhood moral clichés are considered and then surpassed by higher invitations. Do you see yourself as upright because you don't murder people? Well, what about your anger issues? Do you love good people and despise your enemies? That's easy. Now go love your enemies! And be perfect 'as your heavenly Father is perfect' (5:48).

This final focus is where Jesus provides the successful life. Success comes by looking to his kingdom and righteousness as our defining ambition in life. It's not about us; rather it's all about the one we love.

Writer

Ron Frost

Ron Frost currently serves with Barnabas International (USA). He travels worldwide as a teacher and ministry consultant. He previously taught historical theology and ethics at Multnomah Bible College in Portland, Oregon, for 20 years.

**Monday
1 January**

Matthew 5:1–12

Catch a blessing

Prepare

Can we ask for Christ's blessings? Yes. He cares for his us, so press ahead! And notice how well he tailors his blessings to life's circumstances.

Read   Matthew 5:1–12

Explore

Sooner or later we have to ask Jesus about the challenges we face in life. Especially in light of his love for us. In the series of blessings we find here – the Beatitudes – Christ's comforting promises are offered to all who need his care.

The first eight blessings (vs 3–10) have a poetic three-part structure: the assertion of Christ's blessing; a distinct character quality; and a matching benefit. The benefit is the blessing, and the character quality is the basis for the blessing.

A symmetrical beauty appears in each blessing. Are we being crushed by life? Be reassured, the kingdom of heaven awaits us. Are we heartsick in this fallen world? The promise of God's own comfort lies ahead. The certainty Jesus offers in each case is that if our struggles are great, his blessings will always be greater.

Do any of these blessings seem especially appropriate to your own life today? If so, receive it with joy!

> 'Blessed are you when people insult you, persecute you and falsely say all kinds of evil against you because of me.'
> Matthew 5:11 (NIV)

Respond

Jesus offers sweet and sour moments, often at once. Yet in every challenge he assures us of even greater blessings: 'Rejoice and be glad, because great is your reward in heaven' (v 12).

Bible in a Year
Genesis 1,2; Matthew 1

Matthew 5:13–16

Tuesday
2 January

Make a difference

Prepare

It's easy to be passive in life and faith. But listen to Jesus: he made you to make a difference.

Read
Matthew 5:13–16

Explore

Jesus knew how to use simple analogies to help us learn and grow. In these verses he offers two common features of life as reminders: plain salt and the simple light of lamps. Salt flavours and preserves food. Light offers illumination and orientation. Each is ordinary, yet they make life work. Both then and now.

Jesus used this pairing of salt and light to offer a single lesson about the life of faith. Salt is useful with food. Lights illuminate rooms. Believers display the Father. And just as the mixed dirt and salt at the bottom of the salt barrel will be useless; or a lamp covered by a box is wasted, so, too, a disciple who doesn't express a devotion to the Father is just as senseless.

Why this lesson? Because many of us feel like we're ordinary. We can be passive because no one really notices us. Yet, Jesus tells us otherwise: each of us is made for a purpose, and when we live a life of faith it causes others to 'glorify your Father in heaven' (v 16).

> *'You are the light of the world. A town built on a hill cannot be hidden.'*
> Matthew 5:14 (NIV)

Respond

As one who knows and loves Jesus, what opportunities is he giving you today? How will he show off his Father through you?

Bible in a Year
Genesis 3,4; Matthew 2

Wednesday 3 January

Matthew 5:17–20

Reaching heaven

Prepare

One key to the sermon is Jesus' approach to the Law and the Prophets – the Old Testament. Track him closely. He doesn't oppose the law; he fulfils it. Local religious leaders, on the other hand, fall short.

Read
Matthew 5:17–20

Explore

How is Old Testament law related to Christian life today? It's a challenging topic that goes well beyond our space here. Yet it's clear enough that Jesus supported the law; and refused to be seen as a critic. His purpose, in fact, was to fulfil the law, not to abolish it.

But that doesn't remove the tension the law raises. While Jesus could fulfil the law, he warned us not to follow 'teachers of the law' (v 20) who don't keep it themselves. In fact, if we hope to gain heaven we will need to surpass their failed approach.

The way Jesus speaks of the kingdom of heaven is intriguing: can you follow him? Some in the kingdom will be 'least' and others 'great' depending on how they regard the law. But the approach to the law offered by Jesus' religious opponents will not achieve heaven. Why not?

> 'For I tell you that unless your righteousness surpasses that of the Pharisees and the teachers of the law, you will certainly not enter the kingdom of heaven.'
> Matthew 5:20 (NIV)

Respond

Jesus himself was sinless – fulfilling the law. Without him we would all be helpless and hopeless; and with him we find rest. Reflect, then: are you trusting yourself, or Jesus? It makes all the difference.

Bible in a Year
Genesis 5,6; Matthew 3

Matthew 5:21–32

Facing reality

Thursday
4 January

Prepare
Do you ever struggle with moral frailties? In today's reading Jesus doesn't offer bland reassurances. Instead he offers the scrubbing brush of direct confrontation.

Read
Matthew 5:21–32

Explore
Jesus uses a set of contrasts, shifting between clichéd truisms and real spirituality. Each starts with 'You have heard that it was said …' and then pivots, 'But I tell you …' The first statements were sound, but the counterpoints touch deeper heart issues: anger, hypocrisy, lust, and marital failure.

Jesus raises the prospect of being thrown into prison (v 25) or of cutting and gouging out the physical instruments of sin (vs 29,30). He was using hyperbole, of course, yet he was also deadly serious. Sin threatens our lives. As much as the religious leaders in Christ's day were too willing to entertain ungodly desires, we must not go there. And if we are there already, we're being called to turn back and seek the transformation only Jesus provides.

Later in the sermon Jesus will say more about the dilemma of entangling sins. For now we need to face reality and take our first steps into the obedience Jesus invites.

> *'But I tell you that anyone who is angry with a brother or sister will be subject to judgment.'*
> Matthew 5:22 (NIV)

Respond
In our life of faith, as in medicine, a sound diagnosis comes before coming to a cure. If you find anything of yourself in this reading, receive it as a gift of God and respond appropriately, ready to listen and act.

Bible in a Year
Genesis 7,8; Psalms 1,2

Friday
5 January

Matthew 5:33–48
The ultimate standard

> 'Be perfect, therefore, as your heavenly Father is perfect.'
> Matthew 5:48 (NIV)

Prepare

Jesus upped the ante on moral righteousness. Instead asking 'what' questions about sin, he asks 'who' questions. If God, our Father, is the touchstone of righteousness, how do we measure up as his children?

Read   Matthew 5:33–48

Explore

Have you ever made a promise and then fiddled it a bit? Is every promise really binding? Or has a person you don't really trust ever asked you for a loan? How do you respond? And when someone has hurt you more than once, do you ask yourself when enough is enough?

In this stage of the sermon Jesus calls us to new standards of morality. As in yesterday's segment, Jesus set the common religious answers of the day – 'You've heard…' – over against his own answers. Follow his cluster of contrasts and notice the pattern. See how his rhythmic set of scenarios press us to apply new and higher standards.

Pay special attention to the final paragraph where Jesus reached his high water mark: we should live as the 'children of your Father in heaven' (v 45). And what's the Father like? 'Perfect.' So, Jesus taught, always make the Father's devotion to you the standard for your own decisions.

Respond

How does the Father view you? Especially after you've failed him? Jesus, who knows the Father's love, assures us of his perfect devotion. And now as you care for others, share the same care he offers you.

Bible in a Year
Genesis 9–11; Matthew 4

Matthew 6:1–4

Saturday 6 January

Which audience?

Prepare
In daily life we often perform for others. We like to be admired for our character, wit, and wisdom. Reflect, then, on what Jesus shares about the Father's personal sensitivity to our choices.

Read
Matthew 6:1–4

Explore
At this stage in his sermon Jesus takes the question of motives in a new direction. And if we pay careful attention we'll find a touching insight about the Father. He actually attends to us like a parent. In any given moment he knows what we're up to and why we're doing it. It matters to him!

Parental imagery is familiar to us. We know how parents are delighted when one of their children does well. And, Jesus tells us, God's title – 'Father' – is fitting. He has a father's heart for us. So picture a young child who offers her parent a treasured toy. How does the parent feel? A big hug is usually in order!

It's this touching awareness that brings transformation. We aren't drawn to God until we realise he is a caring Father – first to Jesus, and then to all of us who love the Son. And as much as we start to live with God's pleasure in view, our attachment to him grows.

> *'Then your Father, who sees what is done in secret, will reward you.'*
> Matthew 6:4 (NIV)

Respond
You may find yourself torn between pleasing yourself, or the world, and pleasing God. As we live to please the Father we will start to gain a new integrity and growing sense of joy. See for yourself!

Bible in a Year
Genesis 12,13; Matthew 5

Sunday 7 January

Psalm 134

Most low, Most High

Today's note is written by Terry Clutterham

> Your ways, God, are holy. What god is as great as our God?
> Psalm 77:13 (NIV)

Prepare
It's simple. The very best thing is living closely each day with a mighty God who knows us, listens to us and cares for us. What a precious gift from Jesus that is! Thank God for his constant, loving presence.

Read
Psalm 77

Explore
The year gone by – how would you describe it? Read again verses 1 to 9 as you think back on the 12 months. When did you desperately cry out to the Lord for help? Even cry out loud? Did he clearly respond to your cries and change things? Or did your prayers seem to hit a brick wall and there was just that cold, lonely, abandoned silence? How low did you go, and how far towards doubting God?

Now think back, as the psalmist does (vs 10–12), to maybe years before, when God did bring amazingly good things into your or your family's life. Search the moments out. Grab them. Hold them tightly. That's the kind of God he is, remember? Now praise him for it, recalling each of those miraculous things, just as the psalmist does (vs 13–20).

Now can you feel confidence welling up in you for the year ahead? Not confidence in yourself – of course not, who knows what you might do? – but in the 'Most High' (v 10). The Highest Supremacy, the Extremely Exalted, the Totally Sovereign, the One who is greater, more loving, more in control, more powerful than anyone or anything, infinitely more than we can imagine.

Respond
Now doesn't that make you feel like singing to the Most High too? Go on then!

Bible in a Year
Genesis 14,15; Psalms 3,4

Matthew 6:5–15

A Father's ear

Monday
8 January

Prepare
Long ago a hypocrite was a masked actor who played a stage role to entertain the audience. As Jesus tells us more about the Father, and about how to pray, we're invited to pray without wearing masks.

Read
Matthew 6:5–15

Explore
As Jesus offers the Lord's Prayer – or, better, the Disciple's Prayer – he uses striking contrasts. One is the preferred place for prayers; another is the prayer's word count; and the third is the expectation a disciple brings to the prayer.

First, Jesus reminds us how the Father is personally devoted to us. So he prefers private places for conversation, not crowds. Second, he reminds us that the Father doesn't need to be educated, so a few brief and heartfelt words are enough for him. And, finally, he already knows our needs, so prayers don't inform him. Instead it's our chance to embrace him as a caring Father.

Notice each feature. We ask God for his point of view; for his continuing providence; for our own moral change; and for his spiritual protection. And we abandon hypocrisy.

> 'But when you pray, go into your room, close the door and pray to your Father, who is unseen. Then your Father, who sees what is done in secret, will reward you.'
> Matthew 6:6 (NIV)

Respond
As Jesus offers us the Father's heart we're invited to find more secret time with him to pray. He's a willing listener who has been awaiting us for a long time. Toss away any masks and enjoy his company.

Bible in a Year
Genesis 16,17; Matthew 6

Tuesday
9 January

Matthew 6:16–24

Life investments

> 'No one can serve two masters. Either you will hate the one and love the other, or you will be devoted to the one and despise the other.'
> Matthew 6:24 (NIV)

Prepare
Jesus raises critical questions about measuring success in life. Have you made sound investments? Are you devoted to short-term personal rewards or to an eternal relationship in heaven?

Read
Matthew 6:16–24

Explore
Given our viewing options today, this reading is remarkably prescient. Jesus asks: What are you watching? Do you prefer soul-darkening options; or those that stir spiritual health? Do you live for outward appearances – like dramatic episodes of fasting – or do you find secret times for Bible reading?

What about your media options? Do you avoid Internet sites that feed destructive appetites? Or is it a secret addiction? And what if we were to have a major financial crisis, with runaway inflation, would your heart investments keep you secure? Jesus was raising these sorts of questions, not to badger his disciples but to invite real growth. He pitched the visible world against the invisible love of the Father.

As he did earlier in the sermon, Jesus held the eye to be, potentially, a major instrument of sin. Yet it only points to his ultimate opposition: the question of love. We either love God or the world. These are two very different investments!

Respond
Jesus poses an ultimate life-investment question here: 'Who do you love?' It's an either/or test – not a multiple-choice quiz. Have you answered him yet?

Bible in a Year
Genesis 18,19; Matthew 7

Matthew 6:25–34

Trust me

Wednesday
10 January

Prepare

In his sermon Jesus pushes his disciples with hard question about priorities. This section offers a crescendo of sorts with God's providence at the forefront.

Read
Matthew 6:25–34

Explore

Let me tell part of my own story here. As a teenage boy, aged 16, I was ready to leave the church. Yet as a parting act I picked up a Bible and read this sermon. Parts were hard to read – I didn't really trust the Father and I was the hypocrite. Jesus was saying, clearly, 'Enough – stop it!'

Two themes struck home in this reading. The first was 'don't worry' – used six times. And I was, indeed, anxious. A friend had died a few months earlier; my family was moving to a distant city; and I struggled with insecurity.

The second was tied to the first: God's providence is evident, consistent, and breathtaking. So trust him. Earlier in the sermon we've read a number of sections that left us dangling – facing problems of flawed faith or hypocrisy, yet without a clear solution. This reading is the solution: we're invited to God's kingdom and righteousness as our sole focus in life. And then allow him to start applying his providence in our lives.

> *'But seek first his kingdom and his righteousness, and all these things will be given to you as well.'*
> Matthew 6:33 (NIV)

Respond

Jesus is both realistic and caring. He knows how hard life can be, and he points to God's obvious care for nature and asks, 'Will he not much more clothe you – you of little faith?' (v 30). It's a compelling call.

Bible in a Year
Genesis 20,21; Matthew 8

**Thursday
11 January**

Matthew 7:1–12

Applications

> 'So in everything, do to others what you would have them do to you …'
> Matthew 7:12 (NIV)

Prepare
In this part of the Sermon on the Mount Jesus turns to more practical items. Do any apply to you?

Read
Matthew 7:1–12

Explore
How do we navigate life as followers of Jesus? Are we expected to be his moral deputies – ready to pounce on other followers who don't measure up? Are we also obliged to share our faith continuously with doubters, even in the face of their growing opposition and hostility? And how are we expected to engage the invisible Father, and Jesus, about daily matters?

Jesus took up the question of mutual correction and applied a variation of the Golden Rule: be ready to receive the sort of justice you administer (v 2)! And just in case we missed the point, he turned to hyperbole – comparing a speck in one person's eye to a plank in the critic's eye.

Jesus also followed up on his earlier promise of God's providence. If any of us need something, just ask! He used a common form of argument from his day: by moving from a lesser case to a greater application. That is, if you behave well towards your own children, 'how much more' will God be gracious? And, once again, he applied the Golden Rule (v 12).

Respond
You may have questions to ask Jesus, or honest needs to be met. This reading invites us to ask, seek, and knock on the door of 'your Father in heaven'. And then relax.

Bible in a Year
Genesis 22,23; Psalms 5,6

Matthew 7:13–23

Friday 12 January

Hard realities

Prepare
Jesus anticipated the problem of dangerous pretenders who would try to join his followers. Notice how he looks ahead to these practical challenges.

Read
Matthew 7:13–23

> 'Not everyone who says to me, "Lord, Lord," will enter the kingdom of heaven …'
> Matthew 7:21 (NIV)

Explore
Jesus wasn't afraid to confront problems. One enduring concern was how to distinguish those with a pretence of faith from those who are truly responsive. What guidance does he offer?

First he warned against being enthralled with numbers. His imagery of narrow and broad gates pointed to his refusal to moderate his teachings for the sake of popularity. As we've seen already, Jesus was devoted to those drawn to his Father, and he labelled this the narrow road. He recognised that other attractions are in competition with God and will usually draw greater numbers.

Second, if a community has both true and false members, Jesus invited discrimination. Grapes come from grapevines. So if thorns keep appearing in some lives, instead of grapes, be suspicious! All who are truly devoted to Jesus and the Father will walk in the paths of that love.

Finally he warned against accepting the thorn-bearing types as true followers even if they've displayed various forms of dramatic gifting. The only true litmus of faith is a wholehearted devotion to the Father.

Respond
Most of us are optimists about our fellow Christians. We readily embrace all those who profess a devotion to God. But cases of 'ferocious wolves' wearing sheep's clothing call for caring discernment (v 15).

Bible in a Year
Genesis 24,25; Matthew 9

**Saturday
13 January**

Matthew 7:24–29

Made to last

> 'Therefore everyone who hears these words of mine and puts them into practice is like a wise man who built his house on the rock.'
>
> Matthew 7:24 (NIV)

Prepare

Product reviews are always helpful and potential buyers are wise to notice them. Here Jesus reviews his own sermon and reassures us of his ultimate reliability.

Read

Matthew 7:24–29

Explore

Jesus concluded his Sermon on the Mount with the analogy of a house built on a bedrock foundation rather than on loose soil. The implication is clear: you can be either wise or foolish as you build your life.

The sermon is a compressed summary of Jesus' most compelling spiritual lessons. At its heart is the Father's specific attention to each of us – 'for your Father knows' (6:8) – and he invites us into a closer and wholehearted relationship. The Beatitudes, where the sermon began, promise deferred rewards to 'those who hunger and thirst for righteousness' (5:6).

Then the sermon moves from broader social topics – murder, adultery, and divorce – to the more intimate human needs of food and clothing. It concludes, very personally (in 7:11), with 'your Father in heaven' giving good gifts 'to those who ask him'! What stands out is Jesus inviting us to dismiss our distant and detached images of the Father in favour of a more intimate vision.

Respond

You may still have doubts about the Father's care for you. If you do, be sure to take up the invitation Jesus offers to ask and seek assurances from the Father. It's an investment God promises to reward.

Bible in a Year
Genesis 26,27; Matthew 10

Psalm 135

Sunday
14 January

Remembering

Prepare
When we pause to remember God's kindness and providential care, worship is likely to follow.

Read
Psalm 135

Explore
The psalmist sets a context for his composition. He seems to be in Jerusalem on a visit prescribed by God and is watching the Temple staff worship. These 'servants of the Lord' lead in praising God and the psalmist resonates with their chants. Notice the praises: God is 'good' and 'pleasant' and he has favoured Israel as his own people.

One feature of his reflection is a comparison of the Lord to various regional idols. He picks it up early, 'our lord is above all gods' (v 5, ESV), and returns to it later on (in vs 15–18) when he concludes with an ironic judgement that all idols are lifeless, and so are the people who worship them.

How, then, do we worship today? Especially as we see people all around us chasing lifeless values and living lifeless lives? Do they ever infect us?

A cure our psalmist applies is to remember Israel's exodus. God defeated the Egyptians and every other enemy along the way. The living Lord defeats every lifeless enemy. And he always vindicates those who trust him. Praise, then, is our proper response to the only living God!

> *For the Lord will vindicate his people and have compassion on his servants.*
> Psalm 135:14 (ESV)

Respond
When we worship we move from mere thoughts to the engagement of our whole soul, with our heart leading. It's our response to God that grows whenever we recall his love for us.

Bible in a Year
Genesis 28,29; Psalms 7,8

Way in to Leviticus 1–25

When God moves in...

Writer

Jon Gemmell

Jon is a pastor, preacher and lecturer. He has been working in Scotland for the last ten years, seven and a half of which have been in Edinburgh.

Leviticus is the graveyard of many Bible-reading plans. Most of us simply skip over Leviticus and move on to the book of Numbers.

We marvel at the epic narratives of Genesis, with the characters and stories we are familiar with. We gasp at the spectacular miracles of Exodus, as God dramatically rescues his people. Then we land in Leviticus. Blood, skin conditions, discharges, purity, prawns, offerings, sacrifices, punishments, priests, feasts and pages full of other seeming irrelevancies.

But, what if I told you that Leviticus was vitally important? That if we study it carefully, it will transform the way we think and the way we live? What if Leviticus could deepen our understanding of God's character, create in us a yearning for holiness and deepen our love and appreciation for the atoning work of Jesus Christ?

The end of Exodus concerns the detailed plans for the Tabernacle, which answers the question of 'where' God's people will worship. Leviticus then answers the question of 'how' God's people will worship.

There is that old adage that the Queen of England thinks that the whole country smells of wet paint. This is because wherever she goes has been recently decorated. People pulling out all the stops to show themselves at their best. Leviticus is the instruction God gives his people so that they will be their best, they will be holy, as their God moves in to live with them. So we are going to read what happens when God moves in.

Leviticus 1:1–17

Monday
15 January

Drawing near to God

Prepare
How can you draw near to God today?

Read
Leviticus 1:1–17

Explore
Leviticus starts with God calling Moses to himself and speaking to him. Throughout Leviticus God speaks to his people 56 times. Our God is a speaking God.

God speaks to Moses at the tent of meeting, the Tabernacle. His people, though, are not to come empty-handed but with offerings and sacrifice. God has made provision as to how sinful people can come into his holy presence. The word 'bring' repeated in this passage comes from the Hebrew verb to 'draw near'. God wants his people to draw near to him, and gives clear instructions to make this possible.

Notice the stipulations that the bull, the ram or the goat must be without blemish. They need to bring a prize specimen from the herd or the flock. God demands our best, not our leftovers.

These offerings make atonement (v 4), literally 'at-one-ment'. Through sacrifice sinful people are brought back together, are brought to be 'at one' with God. These sacrifices are only a temporal placeholder, an object lesson. God was preparing his people for their ultimate climax and fulfilment in Jesus Christ. The ultimate one without blemish, and his once for all sacrifice for us on the cross.

> 'You are to lay your hand on the head of the burnt offering, and it will be accepted on your behalf to make atonement for you.'
> Leviticus 1:4 (NIV)

Respond
Many people think God is far away, uncaring and uninterested. How different the truth is that we learn in Leviticus. God wants us to draw near to him through Jesus. Live today drawing near to God, confident that he draws near to us.

Bible in a Year
Genesis 30,31; Matthew 11

Tuesday
16 January

Leviticus 11:1–12, 41–45

À la carte

> 'I am the Lord, who brought you up out of Egypt to be your God; therefore be holy, because I am holy.'
> Leviticus 11:45 (NIV)

Prepare
In what ways does your faith in Jesus make you different from those around you?

Read
Leviticus 11:1–12, 41–45

Explore
So hyrax and camel are off the menu; so what? What on earth do these seemingly pernickety food laws have to do with us? Our culture is obsessed with food. Cooking shows, diet plans, countless restaurants, obesity and other eating disorders. We are a culture obsessed with food. So while the exact stipulations of these laws may no longer apply to us, the principles God is teaching through them are still important.

God is teaching us three things in Leviticus 11. First, he is teaching us about obedience. Many people try to hypothesise why some animals are clean and others unclean. In the end we must rest on the fact that God has said, therefore we must obey. A maturing believer is one who increasingly obeys God's Word, one who grows in dependence not independence.

Secondly, as God's people obeyed these laws they would be distinct, different and separate from others. Their faith in God, and obedience to him would make them stand out. Whilst we are not called to stand out by our diet, we are still called to be holy, to be different because of our faith in Jesus.

Thirdly, I think God is highlighting his Lordship over every area of our lives. He is interested not just in our Sundays but in every minutiae of life. God even wants us to eat and drink to his glory (see 1 Corinthians 10:31).

Respond
Every time you eat today, think about these themes of obedience, holiness and Lordship.

Bible in a Year
Genesis 32, 33; Matthew 12

Leviticus 16:1–22

Wednesday 17 January

The big day

Prepare

'Hold thou thy cross before my closing eyes' (HF Lyte, 'Abide with me'). Ask God to give you a clearer understanding of Jesus' sacrifice for you.

Read

Leviticus 16:1–22

Explore

The Day of Atonement comes in the very centre of Leviticus, highlighting its importance. Leviticus is also in the very centre of the Torah, so we are at the middle of the middle. This is a key passage.

Notice four things. First, great care needs to be taken in coming into God's presence. Look at the careful preparation Aaron needs to make in performing this service (vs 1–5,11–14). Holiness is lethal when mixed with sinfulness; precautions need to be taken.

Secondly, see how Aaron needs to sacrifice the bull as a sin offering for himself (v 11). Even the high priest falls far short of the standard of holiness needed to come into God's presence.

Thirdly, see the purpose of the first goat (v 15), the sin offering. This goat is killed as punishment for the sin of the people. This goat performs the work of 'propitiation', absorbing God's wrath for the people's sin.

Fourthly, don't miss the purpose of the second goat (v 21). This goat has the people's sins symbolically transferred to it and then it is driven away, performing the work of 'expiation', showing that their sin is now removed from them. Not just 'forgiveness' but 'forgottenness'.

> 'He is to lay both hands on the head of the live goat and confess over it all the wickedness and rebellion of the Israelites – all their sins … He shall send the goat away into the wilderness in the care of someone appointed for the task.'
> Leviticus 16:21 (NIV)

Respond

What wonderful news! In Jesus we have a perfect high priest and a perfect sacrifice. One who not only takes the penalty for sin but also removes the presence of sin. '… so Christ was sacrificed once to take away the sins of many' (Hebrews 9:28).

Bible in a Year
Genesis 34–36; Matthew 13

Thursday
18 January

Leviticus 19:1–18

Be holy, be loving

> 'Be holy because I, the LORD your God, am holy.'
> Leviticus 19:2b (NIV)

Prepare
The greatest commandments are to love God and love our neighbours. Think about what that looks like practically in your everyday life.

Read
Leviticus 19:1–18

Explore
The dual themes of Leviticus 19 are God's holiness and the holiness of his people. Seven times in these 18 verses God reminds his people that he is the Lord (vs 3,4,10,12,14,16,18) and that they are to be holy, reflecting God's holiness (v 2).

Holiness is to be reflected both in their faithfulness towards God and their fidelity towards their neighbour. Holiness is expressed in their worship of God (vs 1–8). It is revering parents and reverencing the Sabbath (v 3). It is about not worshipping idols (v 4), and offering and consuming sacrifices appropriately (vs 5–8). God is holy and his people are to be holy. How are you doing in pursuing holiness in a Godward direction?

There is also a horizontal dimension to holiness which is expressed in verses 9–18. Not just worship of God but also love for neighbour. Generosity is illustrated by caring for the poor and the stranger (vs 9,10), and truthfulness demanded in dealings with others (vs 11,12). God's people are to care particularly for those under them or worse off (vs 13,14), and treat all with fairness (vs 15,16). They are to be forgiving in their relationships with each other (vs 17,18). How are you doing in pursuing holiness in your relationships with those around you?

Respond
What practical steps can you take today to be loving towards your neighbours? Who can you care for? Who can you be generous to? Who can your forgive?

Bible in a Year
Genesis 37,38; Psalm 9

Leviticus 23:1–14

Friday 19 January

Come on and celebrate

Prepare
How good is your memory? How easily do the truths about God flee from your mind?

Read
Leviticus 23:1–14

Explore
It is very easy to forget. The memory of things quickly fade and important things drift into the background. God's people are prone to forgetting important things, particularly who their God is. Leviticus 23 details the feast days that the Israelites were to celebrate in the regular rhythm of life: reminders for the people to stop them forgetting.

The Sabbath (v 3): a regular reminder that God was their creator. In not working on the seventh day, the people declared their trust in God to provide, and looked forward to a greater rest that was to come. *Remember God as the creator of the world.*

The Passover (vs 4–8): celebrated once a year, reminding them of their rescue from Egypt. They remembered how God saved his people from the death of the firstborn and then rescued them from Egypt. *Remember God who has rescued you from sin and death through Jesus.*

The Feast of the Firstfruits (vs 9–14): reminded God's people that he is the one who provides. That it was God who gave them the land and caused its harvest to ripen. It provided an opportunity for the people to give back to God in worship some of what he had provided for them. *Remember God who gives all good gifts.*

> *Every good and perfect gift is from above, coming down from the Father of the heavenly lights, who does not change like shifting shadows.*
> **James 1:17 (NIV)**

Respond
Thank God for who he is: the creator of the world. Thank God for what he has done: rescuing you from sin and death. Praise God for what he gives: providing everything we need.

Bible in a Year
Genesis 39,40; Matthew 14

27

Saturday 20 January

Leviticus 25:8–17

Pressing the reset button

Prepare
What would it feel like to be free, forgiven and have all your debts cancelled?

Read
Leviticus 25:8–17

Explore
The Year of Jubilee was a remarkable year in the life of God's people. It was a year where the economy was reset. A year where debts were forgiven, property was returned and the land rested from farming. It was a year of liberty, redemption and restoration.

The Year of Jubilee was to be a very special year indeed. In Luke 4, in Jesus' first recorded sermon, Jesus quotes from Isaiah 61, and at the end of that quote declares himself to be the fulfilment of the year of Jubilee, the year of the Lord's favour.

It is now ultimately in Jesus that we will be forgiven of our debts for ever and be fully restored.

'He has sent me to proclaim freedom for the prisoners and recovery of sight for the blind, to set the oppressed free, to proclaim the year of the Lord's favour.'
Luke 4:18b,19 (NIV)

Respond
Think about how you would feel as an Israelite who had fallen into poverty. Someone who had sold all their land, sold themselves into slavery and had no hope of getting back on your feet. Think about how you would feel when the Year of Jubilee came around, and thank God that in Jesus you have been given so much more than even them.

Bible in a Year
Genesis 41,42; Matthew 15

Psalm 136

Sunday 21 January

Forever love

Prepare
Are you a grateful person? Pray that God might make you more thankful.

Read
Psalm 136

Explore

Psalm 136 is a unique psalm due to its repeated refrain 'His love endures for ever.' It is a psalm of thanksgiving that helps us focus our mind on who God is and all that he has done for us.

The psalm moves seamlessly from God's character – his goodness, sovereignty and uniqueness (vs 1–3) – on to his work of creation (vs 4–6). It then lists God rescuing his people from Egypt (vs 10–16), and his conquering the land for them (vs 17–22), before summarising and concluding (vs 23–28).

We cannot get away from the singular focus of this psalm that we are to be people who perpetually give thanks to God because his loving kindness is everlasting.

If this psalm gives reason enough for Old Testament Israel to give thanks to God, how much more reason do we have, as those who are assured that 'neither death nor life, neither angels nor demons, neither the present nor the future, nor any powers, neither height nor depth, nor anything else in all creation, will be able to separate us from the love of God that is in Christ Jesus our Lord' (Romans 8:38,39). This is everlasting steadfast love.

> *Give thanks to the God of heaven. His love endures for ever.*
> Psalm 136:26 (NIV)

Respond

Take time to list all the reasons you have to be thankful to God, finishing each one with, 'his love endures for ever.'

Bible in a Year
Genesis 43,44; Psalm 10

Way in to 1 Corinthians 8–10

Living for God and others

Writer

Esther Bailey

Esther Bailey works for Scripture Union Scotland in the Scottish Borders and in Europe Region. She grew up in Zimbabwe, where she trained as a primary school teacher. In 1983, she came to Britain on holiday, met her husband and is still on holiday 34 years later! She and her husband John have two adult daughters.

At first glance it would seem these chapters are not all that relevant to Christians in the 21st century. After all, I don't very often find myself agonising over whether or not to buy meat that might have been offered to idols. However, it is still true that as Christians we are influenced by the decisions others make – if they think it is all right, it must be all right. Or we find ourselves looking down on others – they call themselves Christians, so how can they be doing that! And, whether we are conscious of it or not, others are influenced by the decisions we make.

Paul's overarching advice in these chapters is to live in a way that encourages people to respond to the gospel and to keep on living God's way. In 8:1b, he says, 'While knowledge makes us feel important, it is love that strengthens the church' (NLT). He challenges us to be less concerned about our own rights and freedoms, and more concerned that we do all we can to help others be part of God's kingdom. He reminds us that the spiritual realm is real, and warns us to consider more than just the physical as we make decisions about how to live.

Let's pray that, as we read Paul's words, God will fill us with his love, and take away our self-righteousness, so that we are able to encourage others to live for him more effectively.

Monday 22 January

1 Corinthians 8:1–13

Don't be a 'know-it-all'!

Prepare
What is more important to you – being right or being loving?

Read
1 Corinthians 8:1–13

Explore

I must confess to being someone who naturally sees the world in terms of black and white – something is either right or wrong! I really have to depend on God for his grace so that I don't tread on numerous toes and upset everyone around me.

The Corinthian church seemed to be full of people just like me! They knew that God was the only true God and that idols were mere lumps of wood, stone or metal; they knew it made no difference whether or not meat had been used in a religious ceremony before it was eaten, and so they thought it was nonsense not to take advantage of cheaper meat available in the temple markets.

Paul, however, challenged them to consider the effects of their decision on those who were newer or weaker Christians. People seeing them get meat from the temple might have assumed that they had been involved in idol worship, and that it was all right to sacrifice to idols and worship God. In Paul's opinion, there was no point in being right, if that causes other people to go wrong!

Paul's words challenge me today – in what ways am I so insistent that I am right, that in fact I am wrong, because I have not loved and built up others?

Be careful, however, that the exercise of your rights does not become a stumbling-block to the weak.
1 Corinthians 8:9 (NIV)

Respond

Is there a particular issue you feel strongly about? Ask God to show you his perspective on this matter and to fill you with his grace and love as you explore the way ahead with others.

Bible in a Year
Genesis 45,46; Matthew 16

Tuesday
23 January

1 Corinthians 9:1–18

I've got my rights!

> *But we did not use this right. On the contrary, we put up with anything rather than hinder the gospel of Christ.*
> **1 Corinthians 9:12b (NIV)**

Prepare
Pray that God would make you more aware of the rights of others than of your own.

Read
1 Corinthians 9:1–18

Explore
Many Scottish schools are 'rights respecting schools' – the pupils know their rights according to the UN Convention on the Rights of a Child, and the school ensures that these rights are upheld. But sometimes the exercise of one person's rights undermines the rights of someone else. For example, when someone's right to express an opinion affects someone else's right to practise their own culture or religion, or leads to them being hurt in body or mind; or when there are not enough resources to allow all children to have food, clothing, a safe place to live or a good quality education.

Paul is aware of his rights as a leader within the church and as a preacher of the gospel. However, he chooses to lay aside his rights, so that there is no hindrance to the good news of Jesus being proclaimed, heard and responded to. In this, he follows the precedent of Jesus, who as Son of God has far greater rights; and he encourages us to do the same.

Respond
'In your relationships with one another, have the same mindset as Christ Jesus: who, being in very nature God, did not consider equality with God something to be used to his own advantage; rather, he made himself nothing by taking the very nature of a servant … he humbled himself by becoming obedient to death … on a cross!' (Philippians 2:5–8).

Bible in a Year
Genesis 47,48; Matthew 17

1 Corinthians 9:19–27

Wednesday
24 January

All things to all people

Prepare

How did you first hear of God's love for you? Thank God for people who were prepared to make sacrifices so that you could be brought into God's family.

Read   1 Corinthians 9:19–27

Explore

Paul did not change his message as he spoke to different groups of people – earlier in this letter (1:23) he states that his message is Christ crucified, even though that message is difficult for both Jews and Gentiles to accept. However, here he explains that his methods of sharing that message vary depending on who he is trying to reach.

More than just altering his methods, Paul alters his lifestyle so as not to get in the way of the message being heard and considered. In Acts 21:26, we see him practising Jewish customs, even though he was aware that these customs were not necessary as part of his Christian discipleship.

He is able to voluntarily do this because he is certain of his freedom in Christ. As he says in Romans 8:1,2, 'There is now no condemnation for those who are in Christ Jesus, because … the law of the Spirit … has set you free from the law of sin and death.' He chooses to use his freedom to work hard, and to submit himself to other people's expectations, in order that some people might be saved.

I have become all things to all people so that by all possible means I might save some.

1 Corinthians 9:22b (NIV)

Respond

Think of a family member or close friend who does not know Jesus – what would you be willing to give up, or to do, so that they might hear the gospel? Pray that God would give you motivation and opportunity to share his love with them.

Bible in a Year
Genesis 49,50; Matthew 18

**Thursday
25 January**

1 Corinthians 10:1–13

Learning from the past

Prepare

'History repeats itself. Has to. No-one listens.' ('History Lesson' by Steve Turner.)

Read   1 Corinthians 10:1–13

Explore

My cupboards are full of things I have started but not finished – a knitted cardigan, a tapestry picture, a dress my daughter will now never fit into.

At the end of chapter 9, Paul writes about the need to finish what God has set before us, and the danger of not giving up anything that would prevent us from finishing. Now he uses the example of the ancient Israelites, who had seen a great display of God's love and power as he brought them out of Egypt. They had crossed through the Red Sea – a picture of baptism; they had eaten manna and drunk water from a rock – a picture of Communion. They even experienced the presence of Christ with them in the wilderness. Yet despite all this, they never received the blessing that God really had in store for them – they never reached the Promised Land.

The Israelites failed because they did not keep their focus on God; they allowed other things to become more important to them. Paul warns the Corinthians, and us, not to rely on past blessings and experiences, and not to take liberties with our spiritual freedom.

> *These things happened to them as examples and were written down as warnings for us, on whom the culmination of the ages has come.*
> 1 Corinthians 10:11 (NIV)

Respond

Where is the church today taking liberties with spiritual freedom? How can we learn from the past? What change in focus do we need in order to finish the race? Thank God that he is faithful. Pray that he will provide a way out.

Bible in a Year
Exodus 1,2; Psalms 11,12

1 Corinthians 10:14–22

Friday 26 January

Look beyond what you see!

Prepare
How aware are you of spiritual realities in the everyday world around you?

Read
1 Corinthians 10:14–22

Explore
In Disney's *The Lion King 1½*, Rafiki the mandrill encourages Timon the meerkat to 'look beyond what you see'. In this reading, Paul encourages the Corinthian Christians to do the same.

When considering idols, he has already agreed with them that physically idols are just lumps of wood, stone or metal (8:4). But here he expands that idea – physical reality is not the only reality. We also need to consider what is happening in the spiritual realm.

Eating at someone's table in Middle Eastern culture at that time implied friendship, agreement and unity. Thus Communion is symbolic of our 'oneness' with Christ and our fellowship with each other. Similarly, although an idol itself is nothing, eating at a banquet dedicated to an idol meant expressing unity and agreement with demons who use idol worship to deceive and enslave people.

The Corinthians had boasted of their 'knowledge' (8:1). Here Paul appeals to that knowledge and calls on them to judge wisely (v 15): look at things from a spiritual perspective, don't play with fire, flee from idolatry!

> *For our struggle is not against flesh and blood, but against the rulers, against the authorities, against the powers of this dark world and against the spiritual forces of evil in the heavenly realms.*
> Ephesians 6:12 (NIV)

Respond
Thank God that he has won the victory over all spiritual forces. 'Having disarmed the powers and authorities, he made a public spectacle of them, triumphing over them by the cross' (Colossians 2:15). Recommit yourself to being wholly united to him, and to no other spiritual force.

Bible in a Year
Exodus 3,4; Matthew 19

Saturday 27 January

1 Corinthians 10:23 – 11:1

To sum up…

> *So whether you eat or drink or whatever you do, do it all for the glory of God.*
>
> 1 Corinthians 10:31 (NIV)

Prepare
Look back over the week's readings. What has struck you most from Paul's discussion?

Read
1 Corinthians 10:23 – 11:1

Explore
Paul comes to the end of his discussion about whether or not it is right to eat food offered to idols, and in these verses he sums up:

We are free – but not everything we are free to do is helpful to our spiritual growth.

We have rights – but so do others and we should put their good before our own.

In everything we do, we should be mindful of the effect of our behaviour on other people's faith, and on God's reputation.

Our Christian faith is not a private thing, between us and God. The Corinthian Christians had only been considering 'what is the harm to *me* if I do this or that?'. Paul challenges us to consider what might be harmful, and what might be loving, to others in the choices we make.

The purpose of our lives is not to see how much we can 'get away with'. It is to give glory to God and work for the good of others. And we are not on our own in this – we have the example of other more mature Christians, and the example of Jesus himself!

Respond
As we try to live for God in the 21st century, thank God for the example of Christian leaders and of Jesus. 'Remember your leaders, who spoke the word of God to you. Consider the outcome of their way of life and imitate their faith. Jesus Christ is the same yesterday and today and for ever' (Hebrews 13:7,8).

Bible in a Year
Exodus 5,6; Matthew 20

Psalm 137

Sunday
28 January

Living for God

Prepare
When in your day-to-day life do you find it hardest to live for the glory of God? Talk to God about these issues.

Read
Psalm 137

> *How can we sing the songs of the LORD while in a foreign land?*
> Psalm 137:4 (NIV)

Explore
In our readings from 1 Corinthians over the past week, Paul has been answering the question, 'How can we live for God in a pagan society?' Here we see the Israelites asking the same question.

Clearly some Jews did manage to 'sing the Lord's songs in a foreign land' – the Bible records the stories of Daniel, Nehemiah and Esther among others. In these stories we see individuals wrestling with the issues of living within a particular culture but being distinctively God's people, just as we have to do today.

That said, how do we reconcile verse 9 with a psalm inspired by a loving merciful God? Perhaps the psalmist is crying out for God to fulfil his purposes to judge all evil. Certainly, God takes no pleasure in the death of the wicked (Ezekiel 33:11), much less the weak and defenceless (Psalm 82:3,4).

How horrified are we when we see sin in the world? How distinct are we as children of God in our world? How committed are we to seeking God's kingdom and his righteousness?

Respond
'Restore, O Lord, the honour of Your name, In works of sovereign power come shake the earth again … And in Your anger, Lord, remember mercy.'
(Graham Kendrick, Chris Rolinson; Copyright © 1981 Thankyou Music)

Bible in a Year
Exodus 7,8; Psalms 13,14

Scripture Union

SHARING THE GOOD NEWS WITH THE NEXT GENERATION

Eight new booklets from Scripture Union
available in packs of ten for £5 each

BOOKLETS FOR 5–8s

THE BIGGEST SURPRISE

What do you believe? | Who is the light? | THE BEST PRESENT EVER

BOOKLETS FOR 8–11s

THE MOST MIND-BOGGLING MYSTERY!

WHAT IS BEING A CHRISTIAN ALL ABOUT? | WHAT DO YOU DO WHEN DARKNESS COMES TO VISIT? | The GREATEST GIFT of all TIME

Order from your local Christian bookshop | Order from Scripture Union: 01908 856006 | Order online www.scriptureunion.org.u

Way in to Matthew 8–10

What kind of man is this?

For the next two weeks our Bible readings return to Matthew's Gospel, where we join Jesus, his band of close followers and a large crowd drawn from many districts within the first-century Roman province of Syria Palaestina (Matthew 4:25). The action takes place in a limited geographical area around the Sea of Galilee and shows Jesus interacting with a broad cross-section of the region's population.

As we explore these chapters, keep an eye out for the reactions to Jesus from the crowd as well as from individuals.

Jesus often did the unexpected which prompted the disciples to ask, 'What kind of man is this?' (Matthew 8:27). As we rediscover Jesus in Matthew's Gospel, I hope we will be able to answer that question. We may need to discard notions of Jesus that we have absorbed from our culture's portrayal of him and redraw our understanding in line with the Jesus that Matthew presents.

We may discover an unconventional Jesus with a novel teaching style, who does things no one else has ever done and certainly does things no self-respecting rabbi would do. We may find Matthew's Jesus controversial and uncompromising.

Matthew's Jesus certainly walks, talks and breathes compassion. He is generous with his time and attention, caring more for the well-being of individuals than for the adulation of the crowd. I have discovered a Jesus who manages to be authoritative without throwing his weight around, who commands respect, expects utter devotion, yet spends his time serving the needs of others. He is simply wonderful.

Writer

Penny Boshoff

Penny is married to Andrew and lives in Kent with their three teenagers, rabbit and dog. She is a member of the 4 O'Clock Church in Sevenoaks, and teaches at a local school.

Monday 29 January

Matthew 8:1–13

In desperation

> *Jesus reached out his hand and touched the man. 'I am willing,' he said. 'Be clean!' Immediately he was cleansed of his leprosy.*
> Matthew 8:3 (NIV)

Prepare
What do you long for? Do you believe God would give that to you? Whatever your answer, invite the Holy Spirit to give you greater understanding of Christ and to deepen your belief in him.

Read
Matthew 8:1–13

Explore
In Jesus' day, leprosy was an incurable disease with devastating physical and social consequences. Leprosy sufferers were ceremonially unclean (Leviticus 14:2–32), excluded from the religious life of their community, and they were forced to suffer and die away from their loved ones.

Life couldn't get any tougher for this man with leprosy. Imagine the expressions in the crowd as the man approaches. Imagine the desperation driving him forward to Jesus. He believes that Jesus has the power to do the impossible and transform his situation but deep down there is a dull, nagging doubt – '… if you are willing' (v 2). Will Jesus want to help him? Many in the crowd, possibly even the man himself, may have believed that the disease was a consequence of personal sin (see John 9:1,2). If the God of the Old Testament law rejected him as unclean, wouldn't Jesus do the same?

Gloriously, Jesus' answer and actions proclaim something new (v 3). He is willing to touch the unclean to make them whole. Through Jesus, God deals with sin-sickness. Instead of being sent away from God's presence, outcasts (vs 10–12) who trust Jesus are restored and welcomed by God.

Respond
Reflect on all that Jesus has been willing to do to make you whole.

Bible in a Year
Exodus 9,10; Matthew 21

Matthew 8:14–22

Tuesday 30 January

Who do you follow?

Prepare
Think about how you address Jesus (Lord, King, Master, Saviour). How does the way you approach him reflect your relationship with him?

Read
Matthew 8:14–22

Explore
As I write, the twittersphere is full of debate about the US president's type of leadership. The choice of a leader has far-reaching consequences. Who we choose to follow matters deeply. What adjectives would describe your ideal leader? What kind of a leader do you see in Matthew 8?

Jesus was already attracting large crowds (8:1,16,18). His teachings were inspirational (chs 5–7), his new style (7:28,29) challenged the status quo but his words were not 'blessed thoughts'. His command had re-creative power (v 3). One word from Jesus transformed people's lives (vs 8,13,16). Here was a leader with integrity: the compassionate Jesus seen in public (vs 3,7) was the same behind closed doors (v 14). He had time for everyone (compatriot *and* foreigner, male *and* female). No wonder people were lining up to join his band of disciples (v 19). Jesus' enigmatic responses to the two would-be followers remind us that we follow Jesus on *his* terms not our own. He expects us to understand and accept the costs of following him (v 20) and not let anything else get in the way (v 22).

> … many who were demon-possessed were brought to him, and he drove out the spirits with a word and healed all who were ill. This was to fulfil what was spoken through the prophet Isaiah: 'He took up our infirmities and bore our diseases.'
>
> Matthew 8:16,17 (NIV)

Respond
Talk with God about any difficulties or distractions you are facing as a follower of Jesus. Pray for Christians who are finding the cost of following too much to bear.

Bible in a Year
Exodus 11,12; Matthew 22

Wednesday 31 January

Matthew 8:23–27

When the storm strikes

> He replied, 'You of little faith, why are you so afraid?' Then he got up and rebuked the winds and the waves, and it was completely calm.
>
> Matthew 8:26 (NIV)

Prepare
Lay your fears before God. Examine them prayerfully with him. Listen to the Spirit's voice. What does he tell you about God's perspective on each fear that you name?

Read
Matthew 8:23–27

Explore
How do we handle adversity? What do we do when situations threaten to overwhelm us?

Experienced fishermen like Peter, Andrew, James and John would have known what conditions their boats could handle. If they felt they were in immediate danger, they would have employed their considerable skill and experience to get themselves through the storm. This storm, however, had defeated them (v 25), so they call on Jesus. At what point in our own times of adversity do we turn to Jesus?

The disciples believe that Jesus can save them, so why does Jesus seem to rebuke them for their tiny faith (v 26)? Could it be that though they knew Jesus had great power, a doubt remained in their hearts about whether Jesus had power for this particular situation?

What would Jesus say about my faith, and yours? We have the benefit of the Gospel accounts so we see that Jesus has power over disease, nature, death. We know that Immanuel ('God with us') was in the boat with those quaking men. If we know all this, surely we should face adversity fearlessly. The Lord *is* with us in all of life's storms. He is *able* to bring us through every adversity.

Respond
'Lord, train me each day to focus on your love, your presence and your power so that I am prepared to trust you fearlessly in times of trouble. Amen.'

Bible in a Year
Exodus 13,14; Matthew 23

Matthew 8:28–34

**Thursday
1 February**

One word

Prepare
Reflect on your recent topics of prayer. Are there any situations that you hesitate to bring to God? Consider why you may be hesitating.

Read
Matthew 8:28–34

Explore
Jesus was a Jew, his followers were Jewish, his teachings were all based on Jewish Scripture and he spent his whole life in Israel with the exception of a few forays into Gentile areas surrounding Israel, like Gadara (v 28), one of the Greek towns of the Decapolis. So is Jesus' power limited to Jewish borders? Is his authority limited to the human sphere? This passage answers with a resounding 'no' on both counts.

Matthew's Gospel focuses on the demons rather than the poor men inhabited by these dark forces. It is the demons who speak (v 31), addressing Jesus with a Messianic title. Despite their noise (v 29) they are fearful (they know their power and their time is limited) and subservient (they acknowledge Jesus' complete authority over them).

Jesus utters one word (v 32). One word and demons flee.

There is no parity of power, no battle between the forces of good and evil. Jesus has ultimate and complete authority. How does this truth about Jesus give us hope in the face of the destructive forces of evil in our world?

> *He said to them, 'Go!' So they came out and went into the pigs, and the whole herd rushed down the steep bank into the lake and died in the water.*
> Matthew 8:32 (NIV)

Respond
Pray, trusting in the power of the Sovereign Lord Jesus, for current situations where evil seems to have taken hold.

Bible in a Year
Exodus 15,16; Psalms 15,16

Friday
2 February

Matthew 9:1–8

Who can forgive?

> 'Take heart, son; your sins are forgiven.'
> Matthew 9:2b (NIV)

Prepare
'Search me God, and know my heart … See if there is any offensive way in me, and lead me in the way everlasting.' Amen (Psalm 139:23a,24).

Read   Matthew 9:1–8

Explore
There was a prevailing belief in Jesus' time that illness or disaster was a consequence of individual or communal sin (John 9:2; Luke 13:2–4). Perhaps this was in the men's minds as they brought their friend to Jesus. Perhaps the man himself thought that his sin was responsible for his situation.

Whatever the problem, whatever the cause, the men believed that Jesus could sort it out. Who would you bring to Jesus today? What do you want Jesus to do for them?

Jesus doesn't confirm the association of illness with sin, but he responds to faith in him and speaks to the paralysed man's inner fear (v 2), then confirms and demonstrates his power to deal with illness and sin (vs 5,6).

Jesus' authority to forgive sin is the crunch issue here. The teachers of the law knew that God alone could forgive sin (hence the blasphemy claim). What a tragedy that experts of the Scriptures failed to recognise the Messianic signs of Jesus' ministry, so instead of bowing before the Son of God, they stood in judgement on him (v 4)! The crowd's reaction is the right one (v 8). Jesus' authority and willingness to forgive sin should fill our hearts with awe and our lives with praise.

Respond
Hear Jesus' word to you: 'Take heart, son/daughter, your sins are forgiven.' Allow the power of Christ's forgiveness to set you free.

Bible in a Year
Exodus 17,18; Matthew 24

Matthew 9:9–13

Saturday 3 February

The sin-sickness doctor

Prepare

'It is by grace you have been saved, through faith … it is the gift of God – not by works, so that no one can boast' (Ephesians 2:8,9). Praise God for his mercy, his gift, his grace.

> 'For I have not come to call the righteous, but sinners.'
> Matthew 9:13 (NIV)

Read
Matthew 9:9–13

Explore

The grace of God upsets our ways of thinking. From football to politics, national identity to church denominations, we define ourselves by difference. We divide people into 'us' and 'them'. The Pharisees aimed to live righteous lives, by keeping the Law and by distancing themselves from anything and anyone they considered unholy. Tax collectors like Matthew were unholy. They were the despised 'them' (v 10). Not only did they collaborate with the hated Roman regime but they had a reputation for fleecing their own people to line their pockets.

Jesus doesn't keep his distance from those the Pharisees would regard as scum (vs 9,10) because his role is to deal with and heal sin-sickness (v 12). When it comes to sin-sickness there is no 'us' and 'them' (see Romans 3:10). Consider the groups of people who are despised in your country (loan sharks, paedophiles, drug dealers). How might Jesus want his followers today to show mercy to them (v 13)? How might we let them know that Jesus wants them in his kingdom?

Respond

Why not research Christian organisations that work in prisons or with ex-offenders in your area? Consider ways you might support them (through prayer, giving or volunteering); perhaps you could invite others in your fellowship to join you.

Bible in a Year
Exodus 19,20; Matthew 25

Sunday 4 February

Psalm 138

With all my heart

> *I will bow down towards your holy temple and will praise your name for your unfailing love and your faithfulness, for you have so exalted your solemn decree that it surpasses your fame.*
> Psalm 138:2 (NIV)

Prepare
Think of one aspect of God's character that you are truly grateful for. Tell him why.

Read
Psalm 138

Explore
This psalm rings with wholehearted joy for God. There is a certainty about who God is and what he is like (vs 2,5,6) which is based on the psalmist's personal experience of God (vs 3,7,8). This joy is explosive – David can't keep it to himself – it erupts in public expressions of praise and devotion (vs 1,2).

It is natural and fitting when God answers our prayers to praise him for his love and care (vs 1–3). I wonder whether we remember God's love and mercy with such certainty and joy, as the psalmist does here, when we 'walk in the midst of trouble' (v 7)? Very often troubles we face now can make us anxious about the future. David, however, focused his whole attention on God rather than his current problems. Look at all the phrases beginning 'you' or 'your'. As he remembered God's character from past events (vs 1–3), he reminded himself of God's involvement in the present (vs 6,7) and that gave him hope for the future (v 8).

Respond
Make God your focus today. Think about his character, remember what he has done. Use a hymn or song of praise to help you worship. Why not use verses 4 and 5 to pray for God's glory to be known more widely?

Bible in a Year
Exodus 21,22; Psalm 17

Matthew 9:14–17

Monday
5 February

Enjoying Jesus

Prepare
What gives you joy? How would you rate your current 'joy' level in your relationship with the Lord?

Read
Matthew 9:14–17

Explore
The Pharisees and John and his followers took their relationship with God very seriously. Keeping the Old Testament law included fasting on specific days (see Leviticus 23:32). The Pharisees went one step further, fasting twice a week for good measure so they would be ready for God's kingdom. John's disciples imply Jesus' disciples are not serious about God (v 14).

Jesus' reply reminds them and us that a relationship with God is not about following rules and regulations but enjoying God for who he is. Jesus' reference to bridegrooms would have reminded John's well-versed disciples of Isaiah 62:5 where God is compared to a bridegroom. Jesus' point is clear: when God is present with you, enjoy him!

Jesus' reference to wineskins and cloth signalled that God was doing something new. The shadow of the crucifixion lay ahead (v 15) but beyond that new truths would be revealed. When the Holy Spirit was poured out, like new wine, at Pentecost, God opened up a new way to be present with his people always (see Joel 2:28,29).

> *'How can the guests of the bridegroom mourn while he is with them?'*
> Matthew 9:15 (NIV)

Respond
We have every reason to be joyful. The Spirit of the Lord has been poured out on all those who trust in Jesus. He is God's presence with us, giving us new life. Praise God!

Bible in a Year
Exodus 23,24; Matthew 26

Tuesday 6 February

Matthew 9:18–26

No second-class citizens

> Jesus turned and saw her. 'Take heart, daughter,' he said, 'your faith has healed you.' And the woman was healed at that moment.
>
> Matthew 9:22 (NIV)

Prepare
How can you be sure you are valued by God? What evidence has Matthew's Gospel given you so far?

Read
Matthew 9:18–26

Explore
The miracle of healing and new life that we see here are key signs of Jesus' role as Messiah (see Luke 7:22). The unexpected twist lies in who receives these blessings. In the ancient world women were considered inferior to men, inconsequential, useful only for bearing burdens and bearing children. The birth of a boy was a joy, a girl was a woe. Jesus' actions and interactions in our passage today (vs 19,22,25) challenge these notions. In Jesus' kingdom, women and girls are not second-class citizens: he values all people, female and male. How might our words and actions mirror Jesus' priorities? How do our church fellowships show that all are valued in God's kingdom?

A dead girl (vs 23–25) and a haemorrhaging woman (v 20) presented a double whammy of ritual defilement for any self-respecting rabbi (see Leviticus 15:25; 21:1,2)! Due to her bleeding, the woman would have been excluded from the religious life of her community for 12 years. Jesus' gentle words and compassion brought physical and spiritual healing for her and sent a message to the surrounding crowd: mercy is more important to God than adherence to the law (see Matthew 9:13).

Respond
'Lord, help me to value all people – regardless of gender, age, nationality or colour – the way that you do. May my words and actions reflect your compassion for others. Amen.'

Bible in a Year
Exodus 25,26; Matthew 27

Matthew 9:27–34

Wednesday
7 February

King in hiding

Prepare
'Lord Jesus, help me to see you clearly, today. Help me to listen to you and follow where you lead. Amen.'

Read
Matthew 9:27–34

> *When he had gone indoors, the blind men came to him, and he asked them, 'Do you believe that I am able to do this?'*
> Matthew 9:28 (NIV)

Explore
In contrast to yesterday's encounters, Jesus keeps these blind men waiting (v 27). Why? The men have to pursue Jesus and even then Jesus questions the depth of their faith (v 28). So what did they believe about Jesus? By using 'Son of David' (a Messianic title), they were confirming their belief that Jesus was the king described in Isaiah 9:2–7. If Jesus healed them, he would be fulfilling the words of Isaiah 35:5 where the healing of the blind was a sign that God had come to save his people.

Imagine what would happen once word got out that Jesus was Israel's Messiah. Jesus' concern for privacy (v 28) and his news embargo on the healing (v 30) appear to be efforts to control potential Messiah-mania.

The evidence that Jesus is the Messiah continued to mount: the very next miracle (v 32) fulfilled Isaiah 35:6. I've heard people say that they would believe if they had evidence of God. But look at the different responses here: a few people believed and were rewarded for their faith (v 29), the majority were intrigued onlookers (v 33), and some were positively vitriolic in their reactions (v 34). How does this compare with reactions you have received when you have shared the news about Jesus?

Respond
Today, the message of Jesus will be shared privately and publicly – in schools, workplaces and homes. Pray for people to receive Jesus their King.

Bible in a Year
Exodus 27,28; Matthew 28

Thursday
8 February

Matthew 9:35 – 10:16

Meeting the need

> 'The harvest is plentiful but the workers are few.'
> Matthew 9:37 (NIV)

Prepare
'Lord Jesus, work in my mind and my heart today that I might care about the world the way that you do.'

Read
Matthew 9:35 – 10:16

Explore

Jesus' ministry schedule looks exhausting (9:35–38). The scale of the need was huge (9:36,37) and Jesus' humanity had limitations: he could only be in one place at one time.

As Jesus presents the problem to his disciples, he also signals where they will find the answer (v 38). When we see a need which is too big for us to handle we are to pray. Is there a need that comes to mind now? If so, take time to pray about it.

Interestingly, God's ministry solution to the problem was a motley bunch of novices (10:2–4)! Their effectiveness did not lie in their skill or practical experience but in their willingness to act on the spiritual authority given to them (10:1). As Jesus' ambassadors, they were to pass on Jesus' message and do exactly what Jesus had been doing (10:1,7,8).

Tucked in amongst Jesus' instructions to them is a great ministry principle that holds for all Jesus' followers: 'Freely you have received; freely give' (10:8).

If we have heard the good news, how can we help more people hear? What has God given you that he wants you to share?

Respond
'Lord of the harvest, I see people who need your word, your peace, your restoration. Send me and send others in the power and the authority of your Holy Spirit to meet the need and bring glory to Jesus. Amen.'

Bible in a Year
Exodus 29,30; Psalm 18

Matthew 10:17–31

Friday 9 February

Prepared for death

Prepare

'Loving Father, prepare my mind and heart to hear your word. Prepare me for your kingdom. Amen.'

Read

Matthew 10:17–31

Explore

Imagine you are one of the twelve disciples: Jesus has just given you authority to preach, heal and cast out demons. You are eager to get going, to be part of the blind seeing, and the lame leaping. Then Jesus delivers these verses. How do you feel now?

If you follow me, says Jesus, be prepared. Be prepared to be arrested (v 19), betrayed (v 21), hated (v 22), persecuted (v 23), vilified (v 25), killed (v 28).

The book of Acts tells how Jesus' words were fulfilled. But surely Jesus' words are equally relevant for his followers throughout history. Verses 21 and 22 could be written for some Christian believers today facing opposition (even death) from family members, or for Christians in North Korea who face imprisonment if their faith is discovered. As we hear of Christians in Mosul forced to flee or face death, the relevance of Jesus' words (vs 23,28) hits home. Jesus does not offer his followers a prosperity gospel. He promises that, even in dark periods of persecution, his people will be equipped by God's Spirit (v 20) to face opposition. He reminds us that our eternal life is more important than this life – the Christian's soul is safe in the Father's hands (vs 28,29).

> 'But when they arrest you, do not worry about what to say or how to say it. At that time you will be given what to say, for it will not be you speaking, but the Spirit of your Father speaking through you.'
> Matthew 10:19,20 (NIV)

Respond

Visit the websites of Release International, Open Doors or Christian Solidarity International to explore ways you can support the persecuted church.

Bible in a Year
Exodus 31,32; Acts 1

Saturday
10 February

Matthew 10:32–42

Number One

> 'Whoever finds their life will lose it, and whoever loses their life for my sake will find it.'
> Matthew 10:39 (NIV)

Prepare
If you did a time and energy audit of the past week, what might it say about your priorities? Who determines the pattern of each day? Bring your thoughts to God in prayer.

Read
Matthew 10:32–42

Explore
The claims Jesus makes in this passage are extraordinary. The relativists of today might pronounce them outrageous! He claims a unique status before God (v 32) that has implications for all people who hear him, or hear about him (vs 32,33,40). He claims immense influence on earth and in heaven (vs 32–34). He expects people to recognise who he is, to welcome him (v 40), to make him the most important priority in their lives (v 37), to even be prepared to face death for him (v 38).

The disciples had witnessed Jesus' authority over disease, evil spirits and nature. If Jesus is their long-awaited, God-appointed Messiah-King, surely only the highest level of commitment and devotion would be fitting (vs 37–39).

The disciples took Jesus' words to heart (see 26:33–35). But they let him down (26:56). We all do. Jesus did not reject them. Through his death he proved his love for them and us, through his resurrection he proved his authority over all things (see Matthew 28:16–20), and through the coming of the Spirit he proved his ongoing commitment to them and us. The disciples responded with changed lives and priorities (Acts 2). How will you respond?

Respond
'Keep your eyes upon Jesus, let nobody else take his place, and in every hour he will give you power till at last you have run the great race' (Elim chorus).

Bible in a Year
Exodus 33,34; Acts 2

Psalm 139

Sunday 11 February

Known by God

Prepare
God sees you. God knows you. God is with you. Rest quietly in his presence.

Read
Psalm 139

Explore
This psalm is loved by many because it describes so accurately our mix of emotions and thoughts as we contemplate the God who is all-knowing, all-seeing and ever-present.

How do we feel about God knowing us through and through? How do we feel about God seeing us wherever we are (vs 7–10), whatever we are doing (vs 1–4)?

At times, like David, we may feel restricted by God's all-seeing eye (v 5). Knowing that we live in the presence of a holy God may make us want to run away or hide (vs 7–9,11,12; see Luke 5:8; Isaiah 6:5). Knowing God and being known by God can be overwhelming (v 6) and also a great comfort (vs 13–18).

As David contemplates God's omniscience and wisdom, he comes up against that perennial thorn in our faith: why does God not deal with the wicked? The vehemence of verses 19–22 may shock us (we know God's view on loving enemies!), but I know that these words echo my inmost thoughts when I see evil and injustice in our world. Maybe that is why this psalm finishes the way it does (vs 23,24). Our Creator knows us, he is committed to us, so we can trust him to deal gently with our troubled thoughts and our offensive ways (v 24).

Search me, God, and know my heart; test me and know my anxious thoughts. See if there is any offensive way in me, and lead me in the way everlasting.
Psalm 139:23,24 (NIV)

Respond
Meditate on the truth that God knows you completely. Allow it to settle in your heart and mind. Then place yourself in God's hands using the prayer of verses 23 and 24.

Bible in a Year
Exodus 35,36; Psalm 19

Fresh bread, out now!

Don't miss your April–June 2018 issue of *Daily Bread*, available from early March.

Fresh next issue:

Jo Swinney
on Matthew

Mark Ellis
on Numbers

John Grayston
on 1 Corinthians

How to order

- through your local Christian bookshop
- by phone 01908 856006 • by fax 01908 856020
- online www.dailybread.org.uk
- by post Scripture Union (Mail Order) PO Box 5148, Milton Keynes MLO, MK2 2YX
- through your church Bible-reading representative

Or why not subscribe?

See inside the back cover for more details on how to subscribe to *Daily Bread*.

Spotlight on...
the love of God

In *God is Not Great: How Religion Poisons Everything*, the late Christopher Hitchens explained why he thought the very concept of God was repellent:

'I think it would be rather awful if it [the existence of God] was true. If there was a permanent, total, round the clock divine supervision and invigilation of everything you did, you would never have a waking or sleeping moment when you were not being watched and controlled and supervised by some celestial entity from the moment of your conception to the moment of your death ... It would be like living in North Korea.'[1]

As Christians, we know in experience that this is utterly untrue – to know that God sovereignly superintends our lives is not suffocating, but liberating. But why? Doesn't Hitchens have a point? Why doesn't the existence of a sovereign God who creates for his glory mean that we are all mere puppets in a fatalistic game?

In answer: Trinity. The God who reveals himself to the world in Scripture is not a power-hungry dictator in the sky, but a community of persons, united in eternal relational love. In John 17 we catch a glimpse of this relationship: 'before the foundation of the world, you loved me,' prays Jesus to the Father (see v 24). There was love and glory shared between the Father and the Son before the world existed (v 5; see 1:1–3). The God of the Bible is one (Deuteronomy 6:4), yet a oneness of three persons – before there was anything, there was a Father, loving his Son, by their Spirit (see Matthew 28:19). This changes everything.

The Trinity is not three gods, but three divine persons who are who they are only in relation to each other. God the Father is who he is because of God the Son; God the Son is who he is because of God the Father; God the Holy Spirit is who he is because

[1] Michael Reeves, *Delighting in the Trinity: An Introduction to the Christian Faith*, IVP Academic, 2012, p109

Scripture Union Bible in a year syllabus (standard)

January

1	Gen 1,2; Matt 1	9	Gen 18,19; Matt 7	17	Gen 34–36; Matt 13	25	Exod 1,2; Ps 11,12
2	Gen 3,4; Matt 2	10	Gen 20,21; Matt 8	18	Gen 37,38; Ps 9	26	Exod 3, 4; Matt 19
3	Gen 5,6; Matt 3	11	Gen 22,23; Ps 5,6	19	Gen 39,40; Matt 14	27	Exod 5,6; Matt 20
4	Gen 7,8; Ps 1,2	12	Gen 24,25; Matt 9	20	Gen 41,42; Matt 15	28	Exod 7,8; Ps 13,14
5	Gen 9–11; Matt 4	13	Gen 26,27; Matt 10	21	Gen 43,44; Ps 10	29	Exod 9,10; Matt 21
6	Gen 12,13; Matt 5	14	Gen 28,29; Ps 7,8	22	Gen 45,46; Matt 16	30	Exod 11,12; Matt 22
7	Gen 14,15; Ps 3,4	15	Gen 30,31; Matt 11	23	Gen 47,48; Matt 17	31	Exod 13, 14; Matt 23
8	Gen 16,17; Matt 6	16	Gen 32,33; Matt 12	24	Gen 49,50; Matt 18		

February

1	Exod 15,16; Ps 15,16	8	Exod 29,30; Ps 18	15	Lev 4–5; Ps 20,21	22	Lev 19,20; Ps 23,24
2	Exod 17,18; Matt 24	9	Exod 31,32; Acts 1	16	Lev 6,7; Acts 6	23	Lev 21,22; Acts 11
3	Exod 19,20; Matt 25	10	Exod 33,34; Acts 2	17	Lev 8,9; Acts 7	24	Lev 23,24; Acts 12
4	Exod 21,22; Ps 17	11	Exod 35,36; Ps 19	18	Lev 10–12; Ps 22	25	Lev 25,26; Ps 25
5	Exod 23,24; Matt 26	12	Exod 37,38; Acts 3	19	Lev 13,14; Acts 8	26	Lev 27; Num 1; Acts 13
6	Exod 25,26; Matt 27	13	Exod 39,40; Acts 4	20	Lev 15,16; Acts 9	27	Num 2,3; Acts 14
7	Exod 27,28; Matt 28	14	Lev 1–3; Acts 5	21	Lev 17,18; Acts 10	28	Num 4,5; Acts 15

March

1	Num 6,7; Ps 26,27	9	Num 24,25; Acts 21	17	Deut 4,5; Acts 27	25	Deut 21,22; Ps 35
2	Num 8,9; Acts 16	10	Num 26,27; Acts 22	18	Deut 6,7; Ps 33	26	Deut 23,24; Rom 5
3	Num 10,11; Acts 17	11	Num 28,29; Ps 31	19	Deut 8,9; Acts 28	27	Deut 25,26; Rom 6
4	Num 12–14; Ps 28,29	12	Num 30,31; Acts 23	20	Deut 10,11; Rom 1	28	Deut 27,28; Rom 7
5	Num 15,16; Acts 18	13	Num 32,33; Acts 24	21	Deut 12–14; Rom 2	29	Deut 29,30; Ps 36
6	Num 17–19; Acts 19	14	Num 34,35; Acts 25	22	Deut 15,16; Ps 34	30	Deut 31,32; Rom 8
7	Num 20,21; Acts 20	15	Num 36; Deut 1; Ps 32	23	Deut 17,18; Rom 3	31	Deut 33,34; Rom 9
8	Num 22,23; Ps 30	16	Deut 2,3; Acts 26	24	Deut 19,20: Rom 4		

April

1	Josh 1–3; Ps 37	9	Josh 23,24; Rom 15	17	Judg 15,16; Mark 5	25	1 Sam 7–9; Mark 11
2	Josh 4,5; Rom 10	10	Judg 1,2; Rom 16	18	Judg 17,18; Mark 6	26	1 Sam 10,11; Ps 46,47
3	Josh 6,7; Rom 11	11	Judg 3,4; Mark 1	19	Judg 19,20; Ps 44	27	1 Sam 12,13; Mark 12
4	Josh 8,9; Rom 12	12	Judg 5,6; Ps 40,41	20	Judg 21; Mark 7	28	1 Sam 14,15; Mark 13
5	Josh 10,11; Ps 38	13	Judg 7,8; Mark 2	21	Ruth 1,2; Mark 8	29	1 Sam 16,17; Ps 48
6	Josh 12–15; Rom 13	14	Judg 9,10; Mark 3	22	Ruth 3,4; Ps 45	30	1 Sam 18,19; Mark 14
7	Josh 16–19; Rom 14	15	Judg 11,12; Ps 42,43	23	1 Sam 1–3; Mark 9		
8	Josh 20–22; Ps 39	16	Judg 13,14; Mark 4	24	1 Sam 4–6; Mark 10		

May

1	1 Sam 20–22; Mark 15	9	2 Sam 8–10; 1 Cor 5	17	1 Kings 1,2; Ps 55	25	1 Kings 18,19; 1 Cor 16
2	1 Sam 23,24; Mark 16	10	2 Sam 11,12; Ps 51	18	1 Kings 3–5; 1 Cor 11	26	1 Kings 20,21; 2 Cor 1
3	1 Sam 25,26; Psalm 49	11	2 Sam 13,14; 1 Cor 6	19	1 Kings 6,7; 1 Cor 12	27	1 Kings 22; Ps 60,61
4	1 Sam 27,28; 1 Cor 1	12	2 Sam 15,16; 1 Cor 7	20	1 Kings 8,9; Ps 56,57	28	2 Kings 1–3; 2 Cor 2
5	1 Sam 29–31; 1 Cor 2	13	2 Sam 17,18; Ps 52–54	21	1 Kings 10,11; 1 Cor 13	29	2 Kings 4,5; 2 Cor 3
6	2 Sam 1,2; Ps 50	14	2 Sam 19,20; 1 Cor 8	22	1 Kings 12,13; 1 Cor 14	30	2 Kings 6,7; 2 Cor 4
7	2 Sam 3–5; 1 Cor 3	15	2 Sam 21,22; 1 Cor 9	23	1 Kings 14,15; 1 Cor 15	31	2 Kings 8,9; Ps 62,63
8	2 Sam 6,7; 1 Cor 4	16	2 Sam 23,24; 1 Cor 10	24	1 Kings 16,17; Ps 58,59		

June

1	2 Kings 10–12; 2 Cor 5	7	2 Kings 23–25; Ps 66,67	15	1 Chr 22,23; Gal 2	23	2 Chr 13–15; Eph 2
2	2 Kings 13,14; 2 Cor 6	8	1 Chr 1–3; 2 Cor 10	16	1 Chr 24–27; Gal 3	24	2 Chr 16,17; Ps 73
3	2 Kings 15,16; Ps 64,65	9	1 Chr 4–6; 2 Cor 11	17	1 Chr 28,29; Ps 70,71	25	2 Chr 18–20; Eph 3
4	2 Kings 17,18; 2 Cor 7	10	1 Chr 7–10; Ps 68	18	2 Chr 1,2; Gal 4	26	2 Chr 21–23; Eph 4
5	2 Kings 19,20; 2 Cor 8	11	1 Chr 11–14; 2 Cor 12	19	2 Chr 3–5; Gal 5	27	2 Chr 24,25; Eph 5
6	2 Kings 21,22; 2 Cor 9	12	1 Chr 15,16; 2 Cor 13	20	2 Chr 6,7; Gal 6	28	2 Chr 26–28; Ps 74
		13	1 Chr 17,18; Gal 1	21	2 Chr 8,9; Ps 72	29	2 Chr 29,30; Eph 6
		14	1 Chr 19–21; Ps 69	22	2 Chr 10–12; Eph 1	30	2 Chr 31,32; Luke 1:1–38

July

1	2 Chr 33,34; Ps 75,76	9	Neh 3,4; Luke 6	17	Esth 6,7; Luke 12	25	Job 13,14; Luke 18
2	2 Chr 35,36; Luke 1:39–80	10	Neh 5,6; Luke 7	18	Esth 8–10; Luke 13	26	Job 15–17; Ps 83,84
3	Ezra 1,2; Luke 2	11	Neh 7,8; Luke 8	19	Job 1,2; Ps 80	27	Job 18,19; Luke 19
4	Ezra 3,4; Luke 3	12	Neh 9,10; Ps 78:38–72	20	Job 3,4; Luke 14	28	Job 20,21; Luke 20
5	Ezra 5,6; Ps 77	13	Neh 11,12; Luke 9	21	Job 5,6; Luke 15	29	Job 22,23; Ps 85
6	Ezra 7,8; Luke 4	14	Neh 13; Luke 10	22	Job 7,8; Ps 81,82	30	Job 24–26; Luke 21
7	Ezra 9,10; Luke 5	15	Esth 1–3; Ps 79	23	Job 9,10; Luke 16	31	Job 27,28; Luke 22
8	Neh 1,2; Ps 78:1–37	16	Esth 4,5; Luke 11	24	Job 11,12; Luke 17		

August

1	Job 29,30; Luke 23	9	Prov 3,4; Ps 89	17	Prov 19,20; 1 Thess 2	25	Eccl 4,5; 2 Thess 3
2	Job 31,32; Ps 86,87	10	Prov 5,6; Col 1	18	Prov 21,22; 1 Thess 3	26	Eccl 6,7; Ps 95,96
3	Job 33,34; Luke 24	11	Prov 7,8; Col 2	19	Prov 23,24; Ps 92,93	27	Eccl 8,9; 1 Tim 1
4	Job 35,36; Phil 1	12	Prov 9,10; Ps 90	20	Prov 25,26; 1 Thess 4	28	Eccl 10,11; 1 Tim 2
5	Job 37,38; Ps 88	13	Prov 11,12; Col 3	21	Prov 27,28; 1 Thess 5	29	Eccl 12; 1 Tim 3
6	Job 39,40; Phil 2	14	Prov 13,14; Col 4	22	Prov 29,30; 2 Thess 1	30	Song 1,2; Ps 97,98
7	Job 41,42; Phil 3	15	Prov 15,16; 1 Thess 1	23	Prov 31; Ps 94	31	Song 3,4; 1 Tim 4
8	Prov 1,2; Phil 4	16	Prov 17,18; Ps 91	24	Eccl 1–3; 2 Thess 2		

September

1	Song 5,6; 1 Tim 5	9	Isa 15,16; Ps 103	17	Isa 33,34; Heb 2	25	Isa 49,50; Heb 8
2	Song 7,8; Ps 99–101	10	Isa 17–20; Titus 1	18	Isa 35,36; Heb 3	26	Isa 51,52; Heb 9
3	Isa 1,2; 1 Tim 6	11	Isa 21,22; Titus 2	19	Isa 37,38; Heb 4	27	Isa 53,54; Ps 108,109
4	Isa 3–5; 2 Tim 1	12	Isa 23,24; Titus 3	20	Isa 39,40; Ps 106	28	Isa 55,56; Heb 10
5	Isa 6,7; 2 Tim 2	13	Isa 25,26; Ps 104	21	Isa 41,42; Heb 5	29	Isa 57,58; Heb 11
6	Isa 8,9; Ps 102	14	Isa 27,28; Phlm 1	22	Isa 43,44; Heb 6	30	Isa 59,60; Ps 110,111
7	Isa 10–12; 2 Tim 3	15	Isa 29,30; Heb 1	23	Isa 45,46; Ps 107		
8	Isa 13,14; 2 Tim 4	16	Isa 31,32; Ps 105	24	Isa 47,48; Heb 7		

October

1	Isa 61,62; Heb 12	9	Jer 11,12; John 5	17	Jer 27,28; John 11	25	Jer 44–46; Ps 119:49–72
2	Isa 63,64; Heb 13	10	Jer 13,14; John 6	18	Jer 29–31; Ps 119:1–24	26	Jer 47,48; John 17
3	Isa 65,66; John 1	11	Jer 15,16; Psalm 116	19	Jer 32,33; John 12	27	Jer 49,50; John 18
4	Jer 1,2; Ps 112,113	12	Jer 17,18; John 7	20	Jer 34,35; John 13	28	Jer 51,52; Psalm 119:73–96
5	Jer 3,4; John 2	13	Jer 19,20; John 8	21	Jer 36,37; Ps 119:25–48	29	Lam 1,2; John 19
6	Jer 5,6; John 3	14	Jer 21,22; Ps 117,118	22	Jer 38,39; John 14	30	Lam 3–5; John 20
7	Jer 7,8; Ps 114,115	15	Jer 23,24; John 9	23	Jer 40,41; John 15	31	Ezek 1; John 21
8	Jer 9,10; John 4	16	Jer 25,26; John 10	24	Jer 42,43; John 16		

November

1	Ezek 2,3; Ps 119:97–120	9	Ezek 18,19; 1 Pet 1	17	Ezek 34,35; 2 Pet 2	25	Dan 1–3; Ps 132–134
2	Ezek 4,5; James 1	10	Ezek 20,21; 1 Pet 2	18	Ezek 36,37; Ps 126–128	26	Dan 4,5; 1 John 5
3	Ezek 6,7; James 2	11	Ezek 22,23; Ps 120–122	19	Ezek 38,39; 2 Pet 3	27	Dan 6,7; 2 John
4	Ezek 8,9; Ps 119:121–144	12	Ezek 24,25; 1 Pet 3	20	Ezek 40,41; 1 John 1	28	Dan 8,9; 3 John
5	Ezek 10,11; James 3	13	Ezek 26,27; 1 Peter 4	21	Ezek 42,43; 1 John 2	29	Dan 10–12; Ps 135,136
6	Ezek 12,13; James 4	14	Ezek 28,29; 1 Peter 5	22	Ezek 44,45; Ps 129–131	30	Hos 1,2; Jude
7	Ezek 14,15; James 5	15	Ezek 30,31; Ps 123–125	23	Ezek 46,47; 1 John 3		
8	Ezek 16,17; Ps 119:145–176	16	Ezek 32,33; 2 Pet 1	24	Ezek 48; 1 John 4		

December

1	Hos 3–6; Rev 1	9	Amos 3,4; Ps 140,141	17	Mic 4,5; Rev 12	25	Zech 5,6; Rev 18
2	Hos 7,8; Ps 137,138	10	Amos 5,6; Rev 7	18	Mic 6,7; Rev 13	26	Zech 7,8; Rev 19
3	Hos 9,10; Rev 2	11	Amos 7,8; Rev 8	19	Nah 1–3; Rev 14	27	Zech 9,10; Ps 148
4	Hos 11,12; Rev 3	12	Amos 9; Rev 9	20	Hab 1–3; Ps 145	28	Zech 11,12; Rev 20
5	Hos 13,14; Rev 4	13	Obad; Ps 142,143	21	Zeph 1–3; Rev 15	29	Zech 13,14; Rev 21
6	Joel 1,2; Ps 139	14	Jonah 1,2; Rev 10	22	Haggai 1,2; Rev 16	30	Mal 1,2; Ps 149,150
7	Joel 3; Rev 5	15	Jonah 3,4; Rev 11	23	Zech 1,2; Ps 146,147	31	Mal 3,4; Rev 22
8	Amos 1,2; Rev 6	16	Mic 1–3; Ps 144	24	Zech 3,4; Rev 17		

of the Father and the Son. So we don't have three gods, but one God in three distinct persons, who are who they are inseparably in relation to each other, united by eternal relational love.

So what is it like to have our lives ruled by a God like this? Incredibly, John tells us that this glory shared between Father and Son before creation (v 5) is intentionally spread to us: 'I have given them the glory that you gave me' (v 22). The 'them' is not some special elite, but all 'those who will believe in me' (v 20). And the 'glory' he shares is not to do with power or coercion, but self-sacrifice – this is the 'hour' of the cross, in which the Father is most glorified in the Son (v 1).

This is why John could write elsewhere:

'God is love. This is how God showed his love among us: he sent his one and only Son into the world that we might live through him. This is love: not that we loved God, but that he loved us and sent his Son as an atoning sacrifice for our sins. Dear friends, since God so loved us, we also ought to love one another. No one has ever seen God; but if we love one another, God lives in us and his love is made complete in us' (1 John 4:8–12).

The God of the Bible does not desire to control us from a distance, wanting simply our obedience. The God revealed in Jesus Christ is all about love in relationship, and his purpose in the gospel is to draw us in to enjoy the circle of eternally and infinitely joyful unity of Father, Son and Spirit.

Someone has since rewritten Hitchens' words above:

'I think it'd be rather wonderful if it was true. If there was a permanent, total, round the clock divine loving of you, you would never have a waking or sleeping moment where you weren't being loved. From the moment of your conception to the moment of your death and beyond – it would be like living in heaven.'[2]

---

[2] Michael Reeves in numerous apologetics talks given at universities around the UK

Way in to 2 Samuel

Being his

'We leave our day-to-day existence behind when we enter a story – and when we return to the "primary world," as Tolkien called it in an essay called "On Fairy-Stories," we come back altered by the experience' (Frank Rose in 'The Power of Immersive Media').

Everyone loves a great story – a new film that inspires us, a TV box set that relaxes us, a gripping novel that stirs laughter or tears, a sermon illustration that makes us think. As we are drawn in, the story does its work on us, and we are changed – temporarily or, occasionally, permanently – and hopefully for the better.

Now suppose the storyteller is the Ultimate Author – the Lord himself – and the story he tells is not a fairy story – the events actually took place. In fact, it's the story of himself – who he is, what he's like, what he has done, is doing and will do. He tells it to move us and immerse us in it, to shape our lives by it and involve us in it. Then, on his side in what he's doing, we will reflect him to the rest of the world by the way we live and by telling the good news of Jesus the Saviour. So welcome to the book of 2 Samuel. It's the story of God, of David and of us. It takes place around 1000 BC. God is ready to develop the nation of Israel into a community of people who love him faithfully, and David is ready to be king. And are *we* ready to be 'altered by the experience'?

Writer
Terry Clutterham

Terry Clutterham is Director of Digital Discovery for Scripture Union and has wide experience in helping children and young people engage with the Bible. He has long been crazy about helping people explore the full breadth of the Bible and hearing God speak for themselves through it.

Monday 12 February

2 Samuel 1:1–16

I'm committed

> They mourned and wept and fasted till evening for Saul and his son Jonathan, and for the army of the Lord and for the nation of Israel, because they had fallen by the sword.
>
> 2 Samuel 1:12 (NIV)

Prepare

Tell Jesus how much you're committed to him and his ways: 'You're my all, you're the best, you're my joy, my righteousness; and I love you, Lord' (Graham Kendrick © 1993 Make Way Music).

Read

2 Samuel 1:1–16

Explore

Earlier, 'Samuel [the prophet] took a flask of olive oil and poured it on Saul's head and kissed him, saying, "Has not the Lord anointed you ruler over his inheritance?"' (1 Samuel 10:1). What is anointed by God – set apart for his special purposes – is sacred.

The nation is now in mourning for King Saul and his son Jonathan. None feels the pain more keenly than David. He has the Amalekite messenger killed (v 15), either because he has murdered Saul (not as the messenger just reported) or because he has violated the Lord's anointed (v 16). This jars with us – we know not to shoot the messenger, especially one who might just be innocent! But the challenge to us is how ruthlessly David is committed to what God wants – but I'm not advocating, in our zeal for the gospel, that we start killing people!

Every day, through our thoughts, words and actions, we express our commitment to Jesus. This may look odd to some – for instance, thinking the best of people when they have failed, saying kind things in the face of hostility, demonstrating love sacrificially when not bothering would be easier. But who knows where it might lead?

Respond

Let's pray that our 'oddness' will be the start of our friends and family coming to Jesus.

Bible in a Year
Exodus 37,38; Acts 3

2 Samuel 1:17–27

Tuesday 13 February

I'm gifted

Prepare

'Out of the generosity of Christ, each of us is given his own gift' (Ephesians 4:7, *The Message*). Let's thank the risen, ascended, triumphant Jesus for the gifts he has so generously given his people.

Read
2 Samuel 1:17–27

> '*A gazelle lies slain on your heights, Israel. How the mighty have fallen!*'
> 2 Samuel 1:19 (NIV)

Explore

David the songwriter uses his gift to help the nation with its grief (vs 17,18). In particular he expresses his brotherly love for Jonathan, and deep sorrow at his loss (vs 23,26). Read the song again, pausing at the end of each verse to summarise, in your own words, the good things David says about the king and his son. Aren't David's words beautiful?

Notice too where David mentions the Lord in the song. That's right – he doesn't! It's anyone's guess *why* he doesn't. When Christians use their gifts, it doesn't always mean writing poems or music about Jesus, or making a gorgeous meal for the neighbours and slipping in a sermon between the starter and main course. But it does mean using our gifts to point people *in the direction of* Jesus. That's different – think about it! The combination of you, your words, your manner and your gifts should all make a compelling combination.

Respond

Recall the gifts the Lord has given you – the remarkable abilities you often use to help others, within the church and beyond. Thank him for them. Pray that he will empower you to use them ever more generously to express the good news of Jesus.

Bible in a Year
Exodus 39,40; Acts 4

Wednesday
14 February

2 Samuel 2:1–7; 3:1

I'm in touch

> In the course of time, David enquired of the LORD. 'Shall I go up to one of the towns of Judah?' he asked. The LORD said, 'Go up.'
> 2 Samuel 2:1a (NIV)

Prepare

'Show me your ways, LORD, teach me your paths' (Psalm 25:4). Recall a time recently when you believe God guided you. If someone asked you, 'How do you *know* it was God?', what would you say in response?

Read

2 Samuel 2:1–7; 3:1

Explore

Through these events, David appears to be in touch with God and what he wants:

'In the course of time' (v 1). David waits until the appropriate mourning period is over before heading out into Judah and his kingship. He is in touch with the mood of the moment.

'David enquired of the LORD' (v 1). Even though he knows he *will* be king, he still asks the Lord about the timing: 'Is it *now*, Lord?'

'The LORD bless you…' (vs 4,5). The wise leader knows when appreciation really counts, when encouragement is needed and helpful. He treats people in a godly way.

'May the LORD now show you kindness and faithfulness…' (v 6). He assures the people of God's active presence in their situation, now and in the future.

Now, David isn't perfect – as some of the choices he makes later will show – and his motivations here may be slightly skewed, but the Lord is clearly the main driving force in his life. How clear might this be about *us*?

Respond

'May the mind of Christ my Saviour live in me from day to day, by his love and power controlling all I do and say' (Kate B Wilkinson).

Bible in a Year
Leviticus 1–3; Acts 5

2 Samuel 5:1–12

Thursday 15 February

I'm purposeful

Prepare

Look back over the past few years. Can you see how God has made things work together for your sake and for the gospel's? If you can, thank him; if you can't, ask him to show you, and reflect some more.

Read
2 Samuel 5:1–12

Explore

The future plan for a king and kingdom was set out by Moses, hundreds of years earlier. David would know what Leviticus 20:22–24 and Deuteronomy 17:14–20 say, but *we* may need to refresh our minds.

This is the way God wants it to be. So as the trusted leader becomes king, David has the direction of things already laid out before him, with his anointing by the elders of Israel, the capture and establishment of Jerusalem as his capital, and the building of his palace – materials courtesy of friendly neighbour King Hiram. Verse 12 sums up the situation. David sets out purposefully into his reign.

We too can head confidently in the direction we know God has planned, with purpose and boldness, sharing Jesus' grace liberally as we go. Our destination is the Holy City of Revelation 21. As we head there, we will do all we can to get people ready for it, sharing with them the good news of the one who can take them there and helping to eliminate tears, death, mourning, crying and pain wherever we can. That's purposeful living for us.

> *Then David knew that the LORD had established him as king over Israel and had exalted his kingdom for the sake of his people Israel.*
> 2 Samuel 5:12 (NIV)

Respond

We need never wake up and think, 'What shall I do today?' Pray for a sense of urgency to be about our Father's business.

Bible in a Year
Leviticus 4,5; Psalms 20,21

63

Friday 16 February

2 Samuel 6:1–23

I'm worshipful

> David was afraid of the LORD that day and said, 'How can the ark of the LORD ever come to me?'
>
> 2 Samuel 6:9 (NIV)

Prepare

'I'm coming back to the heart of worship and it's all about you, it's all about you, Jesus' (Matt Redman © Birdwing Music/Thankyou Music Ltd). Raise up Jesus in your praise. Draw close to him as you read the Bible today.

Read 2 Samuel 6:1–23

Explore

I've often had to remind myself of one thing over and over again – it's all about Jesus, not me. I slip easily into selfish ways, thinking the world revolves around me, or *should* do. Yet really my life's motivation is Jesus and making him known, through all I am, say and do.

Having set up Jerusalem as his capital, it's obvious to King David that he needs to move the most precious worship object there, isn't it? To remind people of the Lord's presence with them? To show everyone that he's God's man? David doesn't seem to consult with God or others about it – he just decides to do it. So who do you think is really at the heart of all this activity – David or the Lord? Or can it somehow be both?

Then Uzzah takes the hit (v 7). It just doesn't seem right or fair. He's only trying to help! But somehow this isn't the way God wants things to be. Maybe it was about God's holiness or his not needing help, or about ignoring previous instructions from the Lord about how to transport the ark. We simply *can't* place ourselves at the heart of things.

Respond

As the ark heads towards Jerusalem, David seems to have realised that God is at the heart of the worship. So he danced for God 'with all his might' (v 14), much to his wife Michal's dismay. What might you do today that demonstrates clearly that God is at the heart of things for you?

Bible in a Year
Leviticus 6,7; Acts 6

2 Samuel 7:1–17

Saturday 17 February

I'm secure

Prepare

'Jesus Christ is the same yesterday and today and for ever' (Hebrews 13:8). The secret to sharing the good news effectively and contagiously is, in your own life, to overflow with love and thanks to God for Jesus. Try it now.

Read   2 Samuel 7:1–17

Explore

Through Nathan the prophet God reminds David that he was there and active in David's past – guiding, shaping and protecting him (vs 8,9a). (And he has always been with his people even without a permanent house to live in, right?) What's more, the Lord will be with David and active in his future – providing a home for his people, keeping them safe and making sure that David's family continues to reign long after David has gone (vs 10–16).

In this way David will see clearly who is in charge and in whose safe hands he, his family and nation are living. So he can let go of his aspirations to build the Lord a huge, gleaming temple, and leave it to his son (vs 2,12,13). It's OK – it's not all about him and about what he wants to do. It's all about the Lord, his will and his timing (vs 5–7).

> 'Your house and your kingdom shall endure for ever before me; your throne shall be established for ever.'
> 2 Samuel 7:16 (NIV)

Respond

Thank God for what he has done for you in Jesus, what he is doing in your life just now, and what he has promised for you in the future. Pray that your security and confidence in the Lord himself will make you bold today about taking risks for the gospel, and about letting go of what is more about you than about him.

Bible in a Year
Leviticus 8,9; Acts 7

Sunday 18 February

Psalm 140

I'm kept

> I say to the LORD,
> 'You are my God.'
> Hear, LORD, my cry
> for mercy.
> Psalm 140:6 (NIV)

Prepare
Pray that today's psalm will inspire you to pray and praise God fervently.

Read
Psalm 140

Explore
For David, the bad news just got worse. No one needs people in their life who are violent (v 1), plotting (v 2), war-mongering (v 2), slagging them off (v 3) and setting traps for them (v 5). We're not sure when this all happens to David, but maybe for a king as popular as him it's going on pretty much all the time. For David, it's 'me and God against the world' (v 6).

Read the psalm again, noting all that David wants the Lord to do for him – for instance, 'rescue' him (v 1), 'protect' him (v 1), 'keep' him (v 4). Now rerun it, picking out what David wants the Lord to do to those who are causing him grief of one sort or another – for instance, 'Do not grant [them] their desires' (v 8) and 'May burning coals fall on them' (v 10a). What a contrast!

Of course, we don't know if God answers his prayer straightaway or not. But verses 12 and 13 should be enough for anyone. One day the Lord will sort things out fairly, so there's no need to get fixated on revenge. For now, we know we are 'kept' (v 3), and that, one day, living closely with him will be more than enough recompense (v 13b).

Respond
What kind of song do you feel like singing to God just now? What will you sing about all the hard stuff that's going on in your life?

Bible in a Year
Leviticus 10–12; Psalm 22

Way in to Acts 20–23

Solemnly testifying…

The book of Acts details the continuing story of Jesus Christ – how his resurrection life changed the world, starting with the coming of the Holy Spirit at Pentecost to transform fearful disciples into fearless witnesses. The theme verse of the book, Acts 1:8 (NASB), tells us how this narrative will unfold: 'But you shall receive power when the Holy Spirit has come upon you; and you shall be My witnesses both in Jerusalem, and in all Judea and Samaria, and even to the remotest part of the earth.' Note how this story spreads like wildfire geographically: from Jerusalem to all Judea and Samaria, and even to the remotest part of the earth!

In Acts 20–23 a stirring narrative unfolds, from the remotest parts of Asia Minor back to Jerusalem, with Rome to be the next exciting destination. These chapters describe how the Lord led Paul to 'solemnly testify' about him and the changed life he offers – through a legendary all-night teaching session in Troas, to a summary of Paul's three years of ministry in Ephesus, to his 'solemn testimony' to the Jews in the heart of their beloved city of Jerusalem. As we study these passages, the passion and absolute commitment of Paul to share about the news and power of the gospel of Jesus Christ is riveting and challenging: 'Lord, is my life one of solemnly testifying about you, no matter what people might think of me?'

Writer

Dorman Followwill

Dorman is a senior partner at a global consultancy, and he and his wife Blythe live in Oxfordshire, have five grown children and two grandchildren. Dorman and Blythe have an active discipleship ministry, and love to help others study the Bible for themselves.

Monday 19 February

Acts 20:1–12

All night in Troas

Prepare

Have you ever intentionally stayed up all night? Paul did, passionately teaching through the night in Troas. May we be available to the Spirit to speak through us whenever he wishes – even all night!

Read Acts 20:1–12

Explore

After the riot in Ephesus, Paul departed for Macedonia, Greece, and then Troas. Paul was a 'bondslave of Christ Jesus, called as an apostle, set apart for the gospel of God' (Romans 1:1), and in Acts 20:1–12, we see him living out his identity. In Troas, knowing his time there was short, he used every hour to teach the people of the gospel of God. On the last night as Paul taught into the small hours, poor Eutychus couldn't keep pace, drifted off and fell through the window to his death. But Eutychus – which means 'good fortune' – not only had the good fortune to be raised from the dead that night, he had the privilege of becoming a living illustration of the resurrection power of the gospel of Jesus Christ for the rest of his life! Do you live as if you believe the gospel brings life to the dead? Does it mean life or death to you and your hearer? For Paul, nothing was more important than sharing the good news of Jesus with all who would listen – not even sleep!

> When he had gone back up and had broken the bread and eaten, he talked with them a long while until daybreak, and then left.
>
> Acts 20:11 (NASB)

Respond

Is your identity so firmly in Christ that you would joyfully sacrifice sleep or comfort or respectability, that others would know him? May we all believe and share the gospel as if lives depend on it.

Bible in a Year
Leviticus 13,14; Acts 8

Acts 20:13–24

Tuesday
20 February

In Ephesus

Prepare
How seriously are you taking the Word of God at this moment? Is it your first assumption and your final authority? Is it more valuable to you than your own life? Pray that God grants us the heart Paul had toward his message.

Read
Acts 20:13–24

Explore
In this majestic passage, Luke quotes Paul's final words to the Ephesian elders. To reflect the heart of his three years in Ephesus with them, Paul chose a particular Greek word that he repeated three times (vs 21,23,24). This word can best be translated consistently as 'solemnly testify' in English. It is a strong word of witness, declaring, warning, proclaiming – a passionate preaching.

First, Paul reminded the elders that the whole time he was with them he 'solemnly testified' about repentance toward God and faith in Jesus (v 21). Next, it is the Holy Spirit who 'solemnly testified' to Paul that he would suffer for the sake of the gospel (v 23). But, for Paul, to 'solemnly testify' about the message of God's grace was more important to him than his own life (v 24). What a challenge to us! What drives our lives, our decisions? If this gospel is true, then what impact should it have on the way that we spend our time, and how we speak to others?

> *But I do not consider my life of any account as dear to myself, so that I may finish my course and the ministry which I received from the Lord Jesus, to testify solemnly of the gospel of the grace of God.*
> **Acts 20:24 (NASB)**

Respond
Reflect on Paul's statement in verse 24. In prayer, bring to God your thoughts on the challenge you feel.

Bible in a Year
Leviticus 15,16; Acts

Wednesday
21 February

Acts 20:25–38

Of battles to come

Prepare
Spend a few moments thanking God for his love for you. Ask that he would fill you with his love for others.

Read
Acts 20:25–38

Explore
What an example of how Christians should love each other! This was a sorrowful day for the Ephesian Christians – the last day they would see Paul's face. But Paul doesn't hold back from 'solemnly testifying' (v 26) about a worrying future. These elders needed to be on guard for themselves and their church because in Paul's absence, false teachers, even from within the church, would arise and lead some astray. The elders must be on the alert, caring deeply about each and every believer, emulating Paul's care for them. Notice how intensely and passionately Paul taught them (v 31) – with tears! Where does such love among Christians come from? From knowing that they are the Father's very own possession, purchased by the blood of Jesus, called for a purpose by the Holy Spirit (v 28), living in God's presence, and by his grace (v 32). In short, it comes from God.

Do you care about believers' spiritual wellbeing? Have you spoken with such concern for another's spiritual welfare that you were moved to tears? Paul was like this night and day – may we ask God for such love for others.

Be on guard for yourselves and for all the flock, among which the Holy Spirit has made you overseers, to shepherd the church of God which He purchased with His own blood.
Acts 20:28 (NASB)

Respond
Ask God to give you something of his heart for those he has given you to care for – and then use the words of Paul's prayer for the Ephesians to pray for them (Ephesians 3:14–21).

Bible in a Year
Leviticus 17,18; Acts 10

Acts 21:1–16

Of pain in Jerusalem

Thursday
22 February

Prepare

'Greater love has no one than this: to lay down one's life for one's friends. You are my friends…' (John 15:13,14). Worship Jesus as the one who laid down his life for you. Are you willing to lay down your life to follow him?

Read — Acts 21:1–16

Explore

Back aboard the ship, Paul sails from Miletus down to Caesarea. While in Caesarea, a grizzled prophet named Agabus brought Paul a grave message: certain arrest and pain awaited him in Jerusalem. Notice how all who heard it focused on the danger, but not Paul – he heard in this dire word a word of opportunity! He would land in the hands of Gentiles – the very ones to whom he was called! While everyone else begged him not to go to Jerusalem, Paul understood the purpose of his life: to 'solemnly testify' of the gospel of God to the Gentiles.

How different Paul's focus is from the others (v 13) – willing to suffer imprisonment and worse for the sake of the lost. What similarities to Jesus do you see in Paul's resolve to follow God's purpose to Jerusalem, despite the danger (see Luke 9:51 and Isaiah 5:7)? Because Jesus had laid down his life for Paul, Paul was willing 'even to die at Jerusalem for the name of the Lord Jesus' (v 13).

Then Paul answered, 'What are you doing, weeping and breaking my heart? For I am ready not only to be bound, but even to die at Jerusalem for the name of the Lord Jesus.'
Acts 21:13 (NASB)

Respond

Paul set his face like flint to solemnly testify in Jerusalem, despite dire warnings. Yet he often asked his readers to pray for him to have boldness. Pray that God would give you such boldness!

Bible in a Year
Leviticus 19,20; Psalms 23,24

Friday 23 February

Acts 21:17–26
To a Jewish audience

> *After he had greeted them, he began to relate one by one the things which God had done among the Gentiles through his ministry.*
> Acts 21:19 (NASB)

Prepare
Pray for those you speak with about your faith, whether Christians or not. Ask God to open your eyes to truly understand your audience, so that he may speak through you right to their hearts.

Read
Acts 21:17–26

Explore
In Jerusalem, Paul met James and the original elders to give an account of his journey. Paul related one by one the things which God had done among the Gentiles through his ministry (v 19). Note Luke's careful language here: God was the author of the work, the Gentiles were the fortunate recipients, and the ministry was done through Paul. What an ethos: God first, others next, then us. But Paul was no longer among the Gentiles: he was in Jerusalem. This was an unfriendly cultural context. Even newly converted Jewish believers were suspicious of Paul. So, the elders asked Paul to show respect for their Temple culture, and purify himself, so that all would know Paul lived an orderly life, keeping the Law.

This last phrase must have rankled Paul a bit, having written so eloquently about how we Christians are set free from the Law. But that was not the argument for that moment or that context. Paul acquiesced to their request – out of respect for the culture, and out of respect for the elders. Paul was respectful and culturally astute in Jerusalem.

Respond
Pray that God would grant you eyes to see and ears to hear the culture in which you live, so that you can present Jesus Christ winsomely to those around you.

Bible in a Year
Leviticus 21,22; Acts 11

Acts 21:27–39

Saturday
24 February

Amid a pack of lies

Prepare

Have you ever been lied about, and lashed back in response? It's hard to hold one's tongue amid false accusations, but holding one's tongue until the strategic moment is a supreme skill. May God grant us such skill!

Read   Acts 21:27–39

Explore

After only seven days in Jerusalem, Paul was in a row! Jews from Asia had stirred up the crowd with a pack of lies. They said Paul preached against the Jews, the Law, and the Temple. They even falsely accused him of bringing Greeks into the Temple to defile it. Imagine how Paul, hardly a shrinking violet, had to bite his tongue in the face of these lies! What is most notable here is what Paul did not do: Paul never took on the crowd to defend himself. He let himself be taken, dragged out of the Temple, and even when they sought to kill him, he did not utter a word!

Thankfully God sent the Roman cohort in like the cavalry in a Western. The Tribune (commander of a thousand men) tried to address the crowd, but a thousand accusing voices arose. Paul still said nothing, until the dramatic moment in verses 37–39 when he could speak privately to the Tribune: 'I am a Jew of Tarsus in Cilicia, a citizen of no insignificant city; and I beg you, allow me to speak to the people.' Paul chose his words wisely for the strategic man and moment. His trust in God's purposes allowed him to 'tame the tongue' (see James 3:3–12).

> But Paul said, 'I am a Jew of Tarsus in Cilicia, a citizen of no insignificant city; and I beg you, allow me to speak to the people.'
> Acts 21:39 (NASB)

Respond

Pray for opportunities to 'solemnly testify' about Jesus today, but the wisdom also for the strategic moment.

Bible in a Year
Leviticus 23,24; Acts 12

Sunday
25 February

Psalm 141:1–10

Our Lord who is here!

> For my eyes are toward You, O GOD, THE LORD; In You I take refuge; do not leave me defenseless.
>
> Psalm 141:8 (NASB)

Prepare

The measure of a man or woman is twofold: to whom do they call for help on the day of trial, and on what do they train their focus?

Read
Psalm 141:1–10

Explore

The first word of this psalm in Hebrew – the original language – clearly indicates where David's strength lies. David's first word is Yahweh ('the Lord') – the unspeakable personal and relational name for God, first revealed in Genesis 2:4. So David's first words are these: 'Yahweh I call to you…' David knew the one to whom he would call on the day of darkness. Three times in this searching prayer, David invokes this mysterious divine name: as his first word in verse 1, again in verse 3, and perhaps most revealingly in verse 8 when David cries out literally, 'But on you Lord my eyes…' The measure of David the man was that he called out to Yahweh first on his darkest days, and he riveted his eyes on Yahweh to find a refuge.

When God first revealed himself to Moses as Yahweh, it came with the explanation, 'I AM WHO I AM' (Exodus 3:14). Many see in this name not only the eternal being of the Lord, but also his personal presence. Perhaps we may translate Yahweh this way: I AM HERE. Perhaps his personal name is an eternal answer to our most desperate prayer – 'Lord, where are you?' I AM HERE.

Respond

Spend some time now praying the words of David in this profound psalm, calling out to our Lord in your need, and focusing on him with riveted eyes.

Bible in a Year
Leviticus 25,26; Psalm 25

Acts 21:40 – 22:5

In their language

Monday
26 February

Prepare
Tensions in relationships can lead some to silence and others to aggression. How do you build a bridge to hostility?

Read
Acts 21:40 – 22:5

Explore
In these verses, Paul faces one of the supreme challenges of his life. Once before, he had tried to preach to the Jews in Jerusalem, and he had barely escaped with his life (Acts 9:28–30). Now he stood before the ravening mob once again. How would he build a bridge? How would they listen to him? In a stroke of Spirit-inspired genius, Paul calmly raised his hand to silence the mob, and spoke to them in their own language: the Hebrew dialect. With genuine respect, he began: 'Brothers and fathers, hear my defence…' and, on hearing Paul address them in their own language, silence reigned. God's man had miraculously silenced the murderous mob… the stage was set… and thus the Holy Spirit was unleashed to 'solemnly testify' through Paul his unique story of the transforming power of Jesus Christ in his own life.

Sometimes rather than zeal and boldness, we need patience to wait for God's timing. What looks like zeal for God does not always come from the right heart (v 3). But God's Spirit is with us, just as he was with Paul, and he desires to speak through us, even into the hardest relationship.

> *When he had given him permission, Paul, standing on the stairs, motioned to the people with his hand; and when there was a great hush, he spoke to them in the Hebrew dialect…*
>
> Acts 21:40 (NASB)

Respond
Pray about the hardest relationship in your life at the moment. Ask God to create the right context and give you words that will build a bridge for his love and grace.

Bible in a Year
Leviticus 27; Numbers 1; Acts 13

Tuesday 27 February

Acts 22:6–21

In Jerusalem

Prepare

Have you ever shared your testimony with an audience you know is hostile? Were you tempted to water it down to make it more palatable?

Read

Acts 22:6–21

Explore

This riveting text relates the eyewitness account of one of the most pivotal events in history. With his life on the line, Paul must have been tempted to cut the controversial bits – to tell his story, but not to ruffle feathers. But true to his calling, and true to his sovereign God and Saviour, Paul 'solemnly testified' in arresting detail, with heart-stopping boldness. To the very men who ordered him to Damascus, he told them of coming face to face with the risen Saviour they were persecuting. One can hardly imagine greater drama, but when we get to verses 18–21, the drama actually increases: Paul reported to them the warning Jesus had given him about that specific audience (v 18). Such boldness! But there's no hint of arrogance here in Paul – he confessed that not only was he there at Stephen's stoning, but that he approved of it. This is not a testimony that says, 'I used to be like you, but now I've improved myself'; rather Paul is saying, 'I understand what you think and feel, but God has broken into my life!'

How do you speak about your faith with non-Christians? Is your desire more that they accept you, or that they find forgiveness and eternal life in Jesus? Does your testimony about how you have changed, or about how Jesus had changed you?

> I saw Him saying to me, 'Make haste, and get out of Jerusalem quickly, because they will not accept your testimony about Me.'
> Acts 22:18 (NASB)

Respond

Pray for opportunities to share your testimony today.

Bible in a Year
Numbers 2,3; Acts 14

Acts 22:22–29

Wednesday
28 February

As a Roman citizen

Prepare
What does it mean to be 'wise as serpents and innocent as doves' today? Are you ready to leverage the laws of today to know how best to further the gospel amid adversity?

Read
Acts 22:22–29

Explore
With the mob again trying to kill him, the Tribune had to save Paul's life once more. But Paul was about to go from the frying pan into the fire: the Tribune ordered him to be punished by scourging – meaning to have his skin shredded by a whip with leather thongs into which were tied pieces of broken glass or metal. You would think Paul would say something to save himself from this torture, but he kept silent once again! Only when the scourging was about to begin, did Paul calmly ask a simple question (v 25). Like an expert swordsman with a delicate rapier, Paul cut through another desperate situation and in one masterstroke paved his road to Rome.

In many cultures around the world and increasingly in the West, Christians are under pressure to keep silent, opposed when they speak publicly about their faith, and worse. Do you know what protections the law in your country can provide for Christians? In the UK, the Evangelical Alliance and Lawyers Christian Fellowship have jointly published 'Speak Up!', a resource that outlines the legal freedoms Christians have to speak publicly about Christ.

> *Therefore those who were about to examine him immediately let go of him; and the commander also was afraid when he found out that he was a Roman, and because he had put him in chains.*
> Acts 22:29 (NASB)

Respond
Find out how the law in your country impacts on your freedom to share your faith.

Bible in a Year
Numbers 4,5; Acts 15

**Thursday
1 March**

Acts 22:30 – 23:11

To the Sanhedrin

> But on the next day, wishing to know for certain why he had been accused by the Jews, he released him and ordered the chief priests and all the Council to assemble, and brought Paul down and set him before them.
>
> Acts 22:30 (NASB)

Prepare

'You will be my witnesses in Jerusalem, and in all Judea and Samaria, and to the ends of the earth' (Acts 1:8). Where does your strength come from to be a witness for Christ?

Read   Acts 22:30 – 23:11

Explore

Have you ever been caught between the hammer and anvil – between two opposing parties? Paul was caught between a Tribune and the Sanhedrin, and between the Sadducees and the Pharisees… hammers and anvils everywhere! But while the Tribune stewed and the Sanhedrin argued, God was at work: through the Tribune, God protected Paul and teed up another strategic opportunity to 'solemnly testify', this time at the heart of the Empire in Rome.

Paul's certainty as to the mission Jesus had given him surely gave him confidence, even in such chaos. But so did the experience of the Lord's presence alongside him – 'Take courage', was the risen Jesus' charge to Paul (v 11) when he appeared to him the following night. We may not have had visitations from the risen Christ, but we have the alongside presence of his Holy Spirit (Acts 1:8) who gives us courage and strength. Jesus Christ never fails to encourage us when we need it the most – it is the hallmark of his character.

Respond

Whenever chaos multiplies, our Lord brings order and encouragement, and reminds us he is with us! Take a moment to thank him for standing within us amid chaos.

Bible in a Year
Numbers 6,7; Psalms 26,27

Acts 23:12–22

Friday 2 March

To save Paul's life

Prepare

Ever feel intimidated to step into a messy situation? Maybe you feel too young, too insignificant, or you don't know what to say, or to whom? But pray you will be ever ready to speak the life-saving word.

Read   Acts 23:12–22

Explore

In these verses, a murder plot is thwarted. In the Jews' oath and the chief priests' and elders' collusion, we see evil at work opposing the advance of the gospel. Where do you recognise this in your local context? But then as now, God was at work behind the scenes fulfilling his purposes. This courageous young man stepped into the gap with a life-saving word, revealing the entire plot. There was something about that boy: he 'solemnly testified' to both his famous uncle and to an intimidating Tribune, and secured their listening ears and their confidence.

What holds you back from sharing the life giving word of the gospel? Is it youth, uncertainty of what to say, fear of people rather than God, or something else? Just as God used this young boy – whose name we do not even know – to save Paul's life, God can use every one of us in his work and even save lives for eternity.

> *But the son of Paul's sister heard of their ambush, and he came and entered the barracks and told Paul. Paul called one of the centurions to him and said, 'Lead this young man to the commander, for he has something to report to him.'*
>
> Acts 23:16,17 (NASB)

Respond

It is always easiest not to get involved in sticky situations. But our God did not call us to hold back words of life – we are to 'solemnly testify' whenever he gives us opportunity. Reflect on what opportunities you have to share Jesus today.

Bible in a Year
Numbers 8,9; Acts 16

Saturday
3 March

Acts 23:23–35

To the governor

> 'I will give you a hearing after your accusers arrive also,' giving orders for him to be kept in Herod's Praetorium.
>
> Acts 23:35 (NASB)

Prepare
Has God ever given you a golden opportunity to 'solemnly testify' about him? Have you ever turned away from such an opportunity? Pray that God will make you always ready for his divine appointments.

Read
Acts 23:23–35

Explore
I wonder if this Tribune, Claudius Lysias, ever imagined that his letter to Felix would appear one day in the Word of God? Luke chose by the inspiration of the Holy Spirit to include this entire letter. Why? Because it shows the lengths to which God will go to open curious doors and use unlikely characters to achieve his divine purposes. Jesus had appeared to Paul to encourage him, and to tell him that he was finally bound for Rome – after years of longing and patient waiting (consider Romans 1:9–11).

In order to get Paul to Rome, the Lord unleashed his strategic genius. First he forged a unique relationship between Paul and Claudius: Claudius saved Paul's life no less than four times! Then he sat Claudius down to pen a letter to introduce Paul to Felix. And then, in his kind compassion, he moved Felix to give Paul a room in his official residence: Herod's Praetorium! When God creates an opportunity to solemnly testify about him, he takes perfect care of all the details.

Respond
Paul's life reveals the deep truth Job learned in Job 42:2: '…that no purpose of yours can be thwarted.' May we expect the same mighty hand to open doors for us to solemnly testify of the gospel of God today.

Bible in a Year
Numbers 10,11; Acts 17

Psalm 142:1–7

Sunday 4 March

Crying to one who cares

Prepare

Have you ever been in a cave and turned off your light? Total darkness. Have you ever felt like you live in total darkness, and no one cares for you?

Read

Psalm 142:1–7

Explore

After David's victory over Goliath, and the people's praise that followed (1 Samuel 18), David's life was plunged into total darkness. Saul unleashed his murderous rage and his army on David. To stay alive, David fled to a cave.

From this place, David writes this psalm. There are words of near absolute hopelessness and despair (v 4). David's darkness was isolating. But in the darkness David discovered a quiet person (v 3). He was not alone, and neither is any believer – never alone, no matter the darkness that chokes us. It's this realisation that gives David the strength to pray with renewed hope (vs 5–7), concluding on a note of brilliantly shining hope in the darkness – the God of Israel is for him, and though the present is full of suffering, God will deal bountifully with him. It is our dark times that prove that faith is not simply a matter of believing things about God, but believing that he has blessing – even in suffering – for those who seek him (Hebrews 11:6). What a triumph of perspective and hope… from a cave.

Look to the right and see; For there is no one who regards me; There is no escape for me; No one cares for my soul.
Psalm 142:4 (NASB)

Respond

Everyone someday turns a corner and is plunged into total darkness. If you are there now, or even if not, pray that you will cry to your gracious Lord on that day, and truly find him in your darkness… as never before.

Bible in a Year
Numbers 12–14; Psalms 28,29

Way in to Matthew 11,12

Surprise, surprise!

Writer

Penelope Swithinbank

As an Anglican priest, Penelope has had an international ministry, leading retreats and pilgrimages, speaking on conferences and leading parishes. She is a published author and a spiritual director.

Great stories often have memorable beginnings – like *Harry Potter, Pride and Prejudice, A Tale of Two Cities*. The beginning of Matthew is no exception: 'This is the genealogy of Jesus the Messiah, the son of David, the son of Abraham' (1:1). The significance of those words would not have been missed by the original readers.

Matthew links Jesus with the prophecies and history of the Old Testament; Jewish readers wanted a Messiah, promised by God throughout their history. Currently they were under the oppression of the Romans, ruled over by cruel puppet kings, caught up in rules and regulations imposed by religious leaders. They longed for a king from their own nation, descended from their ancestor Abraham, as promised by God. A king who would lead them in triumphal, liberating war against the enemy. God had promised that help was on the way – and here it is, writes Matthew! *He* has come – the Messiah! But he's not quite what you were expecting, not quite what you wanted, not quite what you hoped for.

As we read about Jesus challenging their expectations, pushing their boundaries, bringing the kingdom of heaven in ways not anticipated, we need to ask: what did Jesus want them to understand by what he said and did? Which boundaries was he pushing, what challenges was he posing? And how does that challenge us today? Where might we need to reconsider what we expect of him? Where does he surprise us?

Matthew 11:1–19

Monday 5 March

Not quite what we expect

Prepare
Use a few moments of quiet for a deep breath in and out, and consciously put aside busy thoughts; pray for the Spirit to help you hear the Lord speaking.

Read
Matthew 11:1–19

Explore

Preparations for special occasions can sometimes be more fun than the event itself. The anticipation, the planning, the delayed gratification, can be wonderful – for example, in our household when preparing for Christmas!

But imagine doing all the preparations yet not knowing exactly what the event looks like, or when, or where. John the Baptist had been called to prepare the way for the coming of the Messiah (v 10) – but without knowing exactly what that would look like. He preached a message of preparation through repentance; people had responded and been baptised (3:1–10). But later, after Jesus had been preaching and teaching for a while, and John himself was in prison, John seemed puzzled and surprised (v 3). Why do you think he sent this question to Jesus?

Jesus had just declared he had not come to bring peace but a sword, which would cause division (10:34–42). What did Jesus say that showed that the kingdom of God was actually better than had been hoped for (vs 4–6)? He doesn't always do what people assume and expect. He brings grace, mercy, healing – and a blessing for those who are not upset by that (v 6).

> 'The blind receive sight, the lame walk, those who have leprosy are cleansed, the deaf hear, the dead are raised, and the good news is proclaimed to the poor.'
> Matthew 11:5 (NIV)

Respond
How might you prepare for the return of Jesus – even though we don't quite know what that will be like?

Bible in a Year
Numbers 15,16; Acts 18

Tuesday 6 March

Matthew 11:20–30

Not quite what we want

> 'My heart is gentle, not arrogant. You'll find the rest you deeply need.'
> Matthew 11:29 (NTE)

Prepare
Think about your own expectations of Jesus. Ask him to show you today what he offers.

Read
Matthew 11:20–30

Explore
Probably most fathers want their daughters to marry well and be loved and cherished. So perhaps people listening to Jesus wouldn't have wanted him marrying their daughter – yesterday's reading ended with him bitterly saying they thought he was Not Quite What We Want, that he drunkenly mixed with undesirables (v 19)! So he berated them (vs 20–24). These are people he knew well – he had lived in Capernaum (v 23; 4:13), and Chorazin and Bethsaida were nearby.

But perhaps they were disappointed in what Jesus said and did? He wasn't what they wanted of their promised Messiah. So they rejected Jesus and his way of ushering in the kingdom; and they chose not to repent (v 20).

Jesus spoke against them in some of the most challenging and judgemental words he is recorded to have ever used. They wanted a Warrior King, but Jesus is a Shepherd King. Look at verses 29 and 30. What words does he use to describe himself and his ways? If you use several different translations, you will find words such as gentle, humble, rest, freely, easy, refreshed, renewal, unforced rhythms, grace, lightly... What is Jesus offering, to them and to us? How does that compare with what you want from Jesus?

Respond
What do your friends and colleagues expect Jesus to be like? How can you help them to see Jesus as he describes himself, and to see what he offers (vs 29,30)?

Bible in a Year
Numbers 17–19; Acts 19

Matthew 12:1–14

Not what we're used to

Wednesday
7 March

Prepare
What are some of the cultural traditions of your church? For example, compare what people might wear to church with what a congregation looks like on the other side of the world.

> '*I want you to show mercy, not offer sacrifices.*'
> Matthew 12:7 (NLT)

Read
Matthew 12:1–14

Explore
Jesus continues causing controversy by pushing the boundaries of what the religious leaders expected. Perhaps we could put ourselves into their sandals: Why do you think they didn't want people to do any work on a Sabbath, such as harvesting grain or healing someone (vs 1,2,10; see Exodus 20:8–11)?

The original command for a day of rest was God-given; but over the centuries the religious leaders had prescribed it in minute detail, stemming from the best of intentions to help people keep the law. 'It's the way we do it… it's what we're used to.' But they had turned what God intended as a blessing into a burden of prescription and parameters. And now Jesus was offering grace and truth rather than grim tradition.

Perhaps it shows that 'religion' is more about doing or not doing, trying to earn favour with God, whereas what Jesus offers is God coming to us in mercy and forgiveness (vs 7,12). He challenged the perceived wisdom of the religious leaders then – might he need to do the same today?

Respond
What would you say to someone who thinks being a Christian means being a killjoy, not enjoying life but following a list of rules and regulations? What might Jesus say to them?

Bible in a Year
Numbers 20,21; Acts 20

Thursday
8 March

Matthew 12:15–21

Not where our hope is

> 'And his name will be the hope of all the world.'
> Matthew 12:21 (NLT)

Prepare
What do you do to escape from pressure? Be honest with yourself. Ask the Lord to help you to trust in the Hope of the World.

Read
Matthew 12:15–21

Explore

There's so much bad news at the moment. I'm under too much pressure – at home and at work. When's it all going to end? Because I'm not sure I can take much more. How can God possibly understand how it feels?

Maybe that's you, or someone you know. But what was Jesus going through? Look at verses 2, 10 and 14. He's been called a drunkard, a glutton, someone who kept bad company. There are death threats, John was doubting him, and now crowds are badgering him (v 15). Jesus was under tremendous pressure – *and* he knew where it was all horribly going to end.

Matthew shows Jesus as the Servant Messiah, described by the prophet Isaiah (Isaiah 42:1–4); the one who gently and lovingly brings healing and restoration. He is the total opposite of those who quarrel and shout loudest and trample over others (vs 19,20); he is the Servant of the Lord (v 18).

No wonder the world will hope in his name (v 21): this is a God who understands. He knows brokenness and pain and frailty and pressure. His name is the hope of the world.

Respond
What pressures are you facing? What difference does it make to know that Jesus faced pressure and opposition? What do you need from the Hope of the World?

Bible in a Year
Numbers 22,23; Psalm 30

Matthew 12:22–37

Friday 9 March

Not what you do

Prepare
How would you define a 'real' Christian? Ask the Lord to show you how to be really real.

Read
Matthew 12:22–37

> 'A tree is identified by its fruit.'
> Matthew 12:33 (NLT)

Explore
Sometimes, Christians are defined by negatives – in my childhood it was a long list including not smoking, drinking, swearing, dancing, playing cards or gambling. And for the Pharisees, it included not doing the unexpected, not challenging the status quo of religion.

But what does Jesus do? The astonishing (v 23). And the challenging. He speaks about transformation from deep inside – again, challenging the perceived view that what you did, how you kept the law, was what God required (v 35). Jesus talks of being fruit inspectors (v 33), illustrating that what comes from the heart shows what the heart is truly like – because it is where every part of life originates.

It's not what we are like – what we say, what we do – at church and on Sundays; it's what we are like the rest of the week – at work, at home, driving on the motorway, stuck in a queue at the checkouts, faced with too much to do and too little time in which to do it. That's when the good fruit (vs 33–37) shows: a real transformation by the power of the Spirit into Christlikeness. Without that, the Spirit is quenched and hindered (vs 31,32). It's not what you do, it's who you really are that matters.

Respond
'If a sudden jar can cause me to speak an impatient, unloving word, then I know nothing of Calvary love. For a cup brimful of sweet water cannot spill even one drop of bitter water, however suddenly jolted' (*If*, Amy Carmichael).

Bible in a Year
Numbers 24,25; Acts 21

Saturday 10 March

Matthew 12:38–50

Not 'til you prove it

> 'Anyone who does the will of my Father in heaven is my brother and sister and mother!'
> Matthew 12:50 (NLT)

Prepare
Sometimes it's helpful to hold out open hands, as a symbol of offering God your whole self.

Read
Matthew 12:38–50

Explore
God, how do I know you are real? Prove it and then I'll believe – how else do I know I can trust you with my life, my problems, my situation?

The Pharisees had similar thoughts (v 38) – although they had already made up their minds that Jesus was not the Messiah they wanted. They had just seen Jesus heal a demon-possessed man (v 22) but they wanted more proof. They got more than they bargained for – the rough edge of Jesus' tongue (v 39)! All he would tell them was that signs would come all in good time – his time. And that they needed to repent and believe in him (vs 41b,42b). The seeking of signs seems to be symptomatic of something else being needed – a healing declutter (v 44).

The Messiah had come but he was not at all what they expected or hoped for, so they rejected him. Jesus exasperatedly uses the sudden arrival of his earthly family to show an enormous contrast of commitment (vs 49,50). To accept him wholeheartedly means a closer commitment of love and loyalty than even that of earthly family ties. Not quite the kind of sign that the religious leaders had in mind when they asked him for one.

Respond
We've seen a Messiah who issues challenges and pushes boundaries, yet offers more than we could ever deserve or hope for. What has challenged you? What does Jesus offer you?

Bible in a Year
Numbers 26,27; Acts 22

Psalm 143

Sunday
11 March

Praying through trials

Prepare

Philip Yancey advised, don't ask *why* this crisis is happening, but *what* is the Lord wanting me to learn through it?

Read   Psalm 143

Explore

This psalm may have been penned when David was fleeing from his rebellious son Absalom (vs 3,4). Another son had raped his daughter, another had died after David's own adulterous relationship (2 Samuel 12). David's life had become a mess, and he requests for God not to judge him (v 2).

The Psalms often poignantly express what we're thinking and experiencing. How does David feel (vs 3,4)? What is his reaction to his fear and depression (vs 5,6)? David turns to God: and it's not necessarily an automatic response to do that in dark times.

David was a great leader, chosen by God, yet how did he describe himself (vs 2,10)? Being a leader, a man after God's own heart (1 Samuel 13:14) does not exempt anyone from tough situations and dark times.

David doesn't actually ask to know God's will. What does he ask (vs 7–11)? And he asks for a quick reply (v 7)! But he uses this crisis to think more deeply about God and where he has seen God at work in the past. He is seeking God, not merely for a quick magic-like solution, but for a deepening of his relationship with God.

> '*Show me where to walk, for I give myself to you.*'
> Psalm 143:8 (NLT)

Respond

David asked God to help him learn to endure and to grow. How does this psalm help in your current situation? How have you come to know God more deeply through past trials? Who might you help to do the same?

Bible in a Year
Numbers 28,29; Psalm 31

Monday 12 March

2 Samuel 7:18–29

I'm thankful

Part 2 of Terry Clutterham's series on 2 Samuel

> 'How great you are, Sovereign LORD! There is no one like you, and there is no God but you, as we have heard with our own ears.'
>
> 2 Samuel 7:22 (NIV)

Prepare

Be aware of sitting 'before the Lord', as David does. What would you like to tell God about your sense of well-being and your frame of mind, as you come to feed on his word today?

Read   2 Samuel 7:18–29

Explore

Some of David's prayer headlines are paraphrased below, as he responds to all he hears from the prophet Nathan. These will prompt our own praise and prayer.

'I can't believe you've done all this for someone like me, Lord' (see v 18b). What is 'all this', do you think? Praise him.

'Your saving power for the people of this country, Lord, and the privilege of being called yours are amazing' (vs 23,24). Pray that more of your own family and friends will become the Lord's people soon.

'I want your name to be on everyone's lips, Lord' (vs 25,26). Cry out to God for this country to be truly Christian, starting with those you live or work with. Pray that even today they'll catch a glimpse of your thankfulness for Jesus.

'Lord, help me to stay true to you forever (v 29), as I know you'll stay true to your promises and to me.' Slipping away from Jesus is all too easy to do. Wrong choices can lead us away from the Lord, as King David will soon find out.

Respond

'The embrace of the Father be the comfort I desire. The name of the Son be the one on whom I rely. The presence of the Spirit be with me every hour. The Three in One be the focus of all I am'
(© John Birch 2016, http://www.faithandworship.com).

Bible in a Year
Numbers 30,31; Acts 23

2 Samuel 8:15; 9:1–13

Tuesday
13 March

I'm motivated

Prepare
'Examine me, O God, and know my mind; test me, and discover my thoughts' (Psalm 139:23, GNB). What do you think God might see when he looks into the depths of your soul today?

Read
2 Samuel 8:15; 9:1–13

Explore
Nice guy, that David – full of love and faithfully keeping his promise to look after Jonathan's family (1 Samuel 20:14,15). All straightforward. Or is it? If David were asking *you* the question in 9:1, what would you think is his motive behind it? Straightforward kindness?

For instance, why does it take David so long to remember Jonathan's family? Does he just want to get Saul's northern tribes back on side? Does he want to show the nation he's Mr Nice Guy and make sure of popular support? Sometimes we question our own motives as Christians.

In my early 20s I recall wrestling often with the thought that maybe I wasn't a Christian after all – I was just trying to be good and kind, and do the things Christians do. The Lord reassured me – I'd definitely said yes to Jesus and the Holy Spirit was changing me. Every Christian has mixed motives, as David may have had. That shouldn't stop us doing great things for the gospel.

> *David reigned over all Israel, doing what was just and right for all his people.*
> 2 Samuel 8:15 (NIV)

Respond
Thank God that when he *does* look into your soul, above all he sees the righteousness of Christ. 'Through the obedience of the one man the many will be made righteous' (Romans 5:19b).

Bible in a Year
Numbers 32,33; Acts 24

Wednesday 14 March

2 Samuel 11:1–27

I'm vulnerable

> *The thing David had done displeased the LORD.*
> 2 Samuel 11:27 (NIV)

Prepare
Ask the Lord to make you alert to the specific details of the events in today's Bible verses, especially to the way in which one error of judgement leads to more and more wrongdoing, and more and more serious consequences.

Read
2 Samuel 11:1–27

Explore
These episodes tell us a lot about the nature of sin, with its root in selfishness. The theme song could be 'It's all about me, Jesus, only me.' For King David, it all starts with a little downtime at the palace when he should be out fighting along with his army. Verse 1 highlights this as a very big deal for what follows.

The thing is, David knows exactly what he's doing. Bathsheba can't say no – he's the king after all. Her husband is away fighting (2 Samuel 23:39), so he won't get in the way. Uriah is loyal to the king, but David doesn't seem to care about that: 'Only me, Jesus, only me.' David has his one-night fling, and knows that can be the end of it (look at the last sentence of verse 4)… except that Bathsheba gets pregnant. Bad gets worse.

It's an indication of the Lord's extraordinary grace and mercy that he uses someone as weak and even deceitful as David to play such a key role in the story of salvation and in Jesus' family tree.

Respond
The Lord is also using us, weak as we are, to bring the message of salvation to those who don't know it. Thank him that he does, and ask for his protection from the selfishness that leads to sin and gets in the way of serving him effectively.

Bible in a Year
Numbers 34,35; Acts 25

2 Samuel 12:1–25

Thursday 15 March

I'm rebuked

Prepare

'Teach me, Lord, to make my life as an offering, to tell the world that Jesus Christ is King, for the glory of God' (Dave Bilbrough © 1990 Thankyou Music).

Read

2 Samuel 12:1–25

Explore

In his book *Restoring Your Spiritual Passion* (Highland, 1986) Gordon MacDonald writes about six important people to have around us to support us in our Christian life, especially when we're in leadership roles. One of these is a 'rebuker' – someone who tells us the truth about ourselves, even though it may be painful for both them and us, someone who will push us to do and be the best. Nathan was a 'rebuker' to David, as well as being a national prophet (vs 8,9).

We Christians need someone in our lives who will look for Jesus in us, and will tell us straight when we're not reflecting him in our thoughts, words, attitudes and actions. Who could that be? Who could we ask? (It will take some explanation!) It should be someone we really trust, who we're sure wants the very best for us and the gospel.

We can never turn the clock back on our wrongdoing – what's done is done, and we (and others) have to face the consequences, as David does (vs 11–14). But we will need someone strong beside us who can help us turn the bad news into good for the sake of the gospel.

> *'The LORD has taken away your sin. You're not going to die.'*
> 2 Samuel 12:13 (NIV)

Respond

'I have sinned against the LORD' (v 13). What would make you want to say this today? Bring it to the Lord in confession.

Bible in a Year
Numbers 36; Deuteronomy 1; Psalm 32

**Friday
16 March**

2 Samuel 15:1–12

I'm a learner

Prepare
'Open my eyes, Lord, to see you beyond the detail.'

Read
2 Samuel 15:1–12

Explore
Like me, you may look at these verses and wonder, 'What on earth have they got to do with my life today with Jesus?' It's the story of Absalom starting, very skilfully, to line himself up in the nation's eyes as their future king. From a little hand-kissing at the city gate to setting up support groups around the country and declaring himself king of Hebron, the rise in Absalom's popularity seems meteoric. So what's to learn?

With tough Bible passages like this, two good first questions are 'How might it help me know Jesus better?' and 'What does it tell us about God, his nature and his ways?' We will grow stronger as disciples (learners) if we wrestle with Scripture like this.

Jesus is at the centre of God's big salvation plan. In some way, these events point to Jesus, the best kind of king, who didn't try to make himself popular by kissing hands – just the opposite (John 6:14,15). He achieved God's purposes by the ultimate sacrifice – of himself killed on a cross.

These events also tell us about God the Father – that he brings about his purposes through people who are sinful like David and Absalom, and like us, and that human failings, plottings and setbacks won't prevent his plans from being fulfilled. He's doing something much bigger, and it doesn't all depend on me.

> *Absalom … stole the hearts of the people of Israel.*
> 2 Samuel 15:6 (NIV)

Respond
Pray that God will guide you in your part in God's history, showing to the world the kind of king Jesus is.

Bible in a Year
Deuteronomy 2,3; Acts 26

2 Samuel 15:13–26

Saturday 17 March

I'm dependent

Prepare

'Enter his gates with thanksgiving and his courts with praise' (Psalm 100:4). Any way you like!

Read
2 Samuel 15:13–26

Explore

Absalom's plot is now clear, and David's onto it. His response is remarkable – under threat, he's organised and decisive (v 14), generous-spirited with those who shouldn't be caught up in the trouble (vs 19,20) and positive (v 22), considering that the crowds tearfully foresee disaster.

David seems more dependent but more confident in the Lord. He leaves the city, palace and fortress behind – they're not safe anyway (v 14). (Remember the water shaft under the walls, 5:8?) He'd rather Ittai, all his men and families stay safe with Absalom, than dragging them in on his side (assuming David's side might be the weaker, vs 19,20). He sends the ark back to Jerusalem – God is with him anyway (vs 25,26).

We're here only because God the Father created us. We live only because he sustains us. We belong to him only because Jesus has saved us. We stay strong only because the Holy Spirit enables us. In our life and our mission to share Jesus, we're totally dependent on the Lord, and that's exactly what we were made to be.

> 'If I find favour in the LORD's eyes, he will bring me back and let me see [the ark] and his dwelling-place again.'
> 2 Samuel 15:25 (NIV)

Respond

Now pray Psalm 62:5–8, with a longing that others will come to know that the Lord is totally dependable in every way.

Bible in a Year
Deuteronomy 4,5; Acts 27

Sunday 18 March

Psalm 144

I'm saved

> He is my loving God and my fortress, my stronghold and my deliverer…
> **Psalm 144:2 (NIV)**

Prepare
Be still and know that he is God, and with you now.

Read Psalm 144

Explore
Psalms are often full of wonderful, vivid images, communicating deep theology and heartfelt response in picture language. Read today's verses again, pausing at each new image as if you're watching scenes from a film.

We don't know exactly what circumstances gave rise to this psalm, but they clearly fit what happens around Absalom's rebellion. Here are snapshots from David's life – the soldier (vs 1,2), the poet (vs 3,4), the musician (vs 9,10) and the shepherd (vs 12–14). Each of these has their own visual expression of what it means for God to be Saviour, our place of strength. For the soldier, it's being properly trained for battle; for the poet, it's thoughts about how much God cares for even little us; for the musician, the latest creation sung on the finest musical instrument; for the shepherd, thousands of safe, well-fed sheep.

Then for me, the best of all – the cinematic sweep God takes from the highest to the lowest to save me – from above the heavens (v 5), down past the mountain tops, through the stormy thunder clouds (v 6), past the battle fields, plunging down into the deepest waters where I'm drowning (v 7). And God grabs me in the nick of time. That image of salvation will stay firmly fixed in my mind. I'm blown away by Jesus leaving heaven and coming to a cattle feed box and a criminal's cross to save me.

Respond
'Thank you, Jesus.'

Bible in a Year
Deuteronomy 6,7; Psalm 33

Way in to Matthew 26–28

God longs to be with us

Writer

Elaine Duncan

Elaine is CEO of the Scottish Bible Society. She is passionate about people growing in their relationship with God through encountering him in his Word.

As we approach Palm Sunday, Holy Week and Easter, we immerse ourselves in the final chapters of Matthew's Gospel. Of all the Gospel writers Matthew includes the most Old Testament references and regularly uses the phrase 'this took place to fulfil…' This has led to the understanding that the original readers were Jews who Matthew wanted to convince that Jesus was the promised Messiah.

Matthew's Gospel would help these early followers of Jesus understand that their identity had changed from being children of Israel to being citizens of a new kingdom. But it is an upside down kingdom. It regularly seems fragile and vulnerable, hanging by a thread. Its King is not like any other king. As the identity of Jesus is revealed as the suffering Saviour we all become clearer about who we are ourselves – sinners in need of this Rescuer.

The events leading up to Jesus' death (the Passion narratives) are not comfortable to read. You may find it helpful to read Psalm 22 a few times over the next two weeks; it is woven into the events in a remarkable way.

Matthew begins and ends his Gospel with the most amazing truth: God longs to be with us. Jesus comes into the world as 'Immanuel (which means "God with us")' (1:23) and he ascends from this world assuring his followers that he is with them always (28:20).

May you experience God with you in new, fresh and tangible ways as you ponder a God prepared to die in your place… that you might live!

Matthew 26:1–16

Was it a waste?

Monday
19 March

Prepare
Have an honest conversation with God about your attitude to money.

Read
Matthew 26:1–16

Explore
Matthew's account of Jesus' life and ministry now focuses on the events leading to his death. Nothing of what is about to unfold is going to be a surprise to Jesus. What do you find reassuring about Jesus' knowledge of events about to unfold (vs 1,2) in light of the scheming of the religious leaders (vs 3–5)?

A nameless woman's beautiful, intimate and generous act of anointing Jesus is a sign of her love and devotion towards him. Jesus sees it as a preparation for what is to come and he commends her for what she has done. In contrast the disciples see her behaviour as an act of extravagant waste. They would have much better plans for the use of this resource.

Jesus' response to them is not uncaring about the poor, but rather a challenge to their perspective and priorities at that point. Was this the tipping point for Judas? It is hard to know what was going on in his mind that led to his betraying Jesus. The juxtaposition of these contrasting views of money at this crucial point in Jesus' ministry is a challenge to us. We should beware lest we 'know the price of everything and the value of nothing' (Oscar Wilde).

> 'Truly I tell you, wherever this gospel is preached throughout the world, what she has done will also be told, in memory of her.'
> Matthew 26:13 (NIV)

Respond
Are you able to entrust your financial situation to the one who knows all things and holds your future in his hands?

Bible in a Year
Deuteronomy 8,9; Acts 28

**Tuesday
20 March**

Matthew 26:17–30

Betrayal and broken bread

> 'This is my blood of the covenant, which is poured out for many for the forgiveness of sins.'
> Matthew 26:28 (NIV)

Prepare

Bring to mind a significant meal you have shared with others. Perhaps someone shared exciting or difficult news. What was the atmosphere like?

Read

Matthew 26:17–30

Explore

Jesus remains in control as preparations are made to celebrate the Passover. I imagine the disciples to be relaxed, enjoying one another's company and happy that arrangements have been made for them to be well fed. Then the atmosphere changes dramatically as Jesus introduces the topic of betrayal. This group have spent three years with Jesus: being taught by him; learning together; working together; trying to figure out what is going on. How could one of them betray him now?

I wonder how the conversation moved on – did the atmosphere remain tense? Perhaps a tense atmosphere was an appropriate context for Jesus to take the central elements of their Passover meal and imbue them with new covenant significance. They were celebrating God's salvation and deliverance from slavery in Egypt. Jesus now shows that he is the one who will bring salvation and forgiveness of sins through his broken body and shed blood. He was broken that we might be whole. He was sacrificed so that we might live. He can see that his death will lead to a glorious new kingdom.

The death of Jesus means that human relationships (broken by betrayal) and our relationship with God (broken by sin) will be forever changed.

Respond

Thank God that in Jesus your sins are forgiven!

Bible in a Year
Deuteronomy 10,11; Romans 1

Matthew 26:31–35

Wednesday 21 March

Weaker than you think

Prepare

God says his power is made perfect (displayed) in our weakness (2 Corinthians 12:9). Can you think of a time when you know that has been true for you?

Read   Matthew 26:31–35

Explore

As Jesus and the disciples move to the Mount of Olives, Jesus gives another warning to them. A different sort of betrayal this time – denial. They will run away from him. They have stuck with him this far, but tonight will be different. In his customary fashion, Matthew shows that this too has been predicted in the Old Testament and quotes from the prophet Zechariah (Zechariah 13:7).

Jesus also says that he will see them again after he is risen. Why do you think this seems to have been missed by the disciples? Were they too distressed by Jesus' prediction of denial? We often miss hearing good news when we are distracted and distressed by something else.

Peter thought he was strong enough to stick with Jesus whatever the challenge. Do you ever get proud of your discipleship? You think of all that praying you do, all those church meetings you go to, the witnessing you do… it boils down to 'God is lucky to have me!' (though we would never put it that way!).

Peter was to learn that we stick with Jesus because of his hold on us, not our hold on him. None of us know how we will react until things get tough.

Peter replied, 'Even if all fall away on account of you, I never will.'
Matthew 26:33 (NIV)

Respond

Pray that in meekness you will find the strength of Jesus.

Bible in a Year
Deuteronomy 12–14; Romans 2

Thursday
22 March

Matthew 26:36–46

Agony

> 'My Father, if it is not possible for this cup to be taken away unless I drink it, may your will be done.'
> Matthew 26:42 (NIV)

Prepare
Quieten your heart to enter the garden with Jesus and his friends.

Read
Matthew 26:36–46

Explore
A garden on the Mount of Olives provides the place where Jesus will do battle with his own will. He leaves eight disciples at the gate and takes Peter, James and John with him. What does Jesus' need for his friends' support tell us about his humanity? He is honest with them about how he is feeling and asks them to pray.

He then moves deeper into the shadows of the trees, alone, to pray. Try to listen to the agony within Jesus. There is an intense struggle going on in his inner being. He knows that death lies ahead, but longs that it would not be needed. What else can he do but plead with his Father?

Consider the implications of this inner battle: the salvation of the world hung in the balance at this point. Jesus wins a victory in this garden. His will is fully submitted to his Father's will.

Matthew's account of Gethsemane describes Jesus living out the prayer he taught his disciples in Matthew 6:9–13. Save us from temptation. Deliver us from evil. Your will be done. Your kingdom come. This is prayer in action.

And there is a loneliness in it. Jesus' friends are unable to stay awake and support him. There are some inner battles we must take to God on our own.

Respond
Sit in silence and thank Jesus that he held his resolve to go to the cross.

Bible in a Year
Deuteronomy 15,16; Psalm 34

Matthew 26:47–56

Sealed with a kiss

**Friday
23 March**

Prepare
In the midst of betrayal and unlawful arrest, Jesus is a man of peace. Are you a person of peace?

Read
Matthew 26:47–56

Explore
The quietness of the garden is now filled with the sound of a mob arriving. Judas appears amongst his friends, but he is only looking for one and when he finds him he says 'Greetings, Rabbi' (Judas never calls Jesus 'Lord') and kisses him. The soldiers move in to arrest Jesus.

Even now we realise that Jesus is giving himself over to this arrest willingly. Think of the many points where Jesus could have walked away, even from the garden a few moments ago. But he is in control, and he knows he is fulfilling a plan agreed within the Godhead.

When one of his followers (John tells us it was Peter, John 18:10) tries to take things into his own hands by responding violently, he is rebuked by Jesus. Although these soldiers are acting on the command of those who have no regard for God and are bent on doing evil, the battle that Jesus is fighting is not 'against flesh and blood' (Ephesians 6:12). Oh that more in our world would take Jesus' words to heart; violence simply prompts more violence (v 52).

As Jesus goes peacefully with those who mean him harm, the disciples flee. This is the point where they desert him. Fear, bewilderment and terror fill their hearts.

> *'Put your sword back in its place,' Jesus said to him, 'for all who draw the sword will die by the sword.'*
> Matthew 26:52 (NIV)

Respond
Lord, 'make me a channel of your peace. Where there is hatred let me bring your love' (attributed to Francis of Assisi).

Bible in a Year
Deuteronomy 17,18; Romans 3

**Saturday
24 March**

Matthew 26:57–68

Where's the justice?

> 'But I say to all of you: From now on you will see the Son of Man sitting at the right hand of the Mighty One and coming on the clouds of heaven.'
>
> Matthew 26:64 (NIV)

Prepare
Think of situations you know where injustice prevails. You may find it helpful to check out the International Justice Mission website (www.ijm.org).

Read
Matthew 26:57–68

Explore
Everything about this first trial of Jesus is wrong from the point of view of justice, and Matthew does not want us to miss the irony. Caiaphas, the chief priests and the Sanhedrin were tasked with upholding Jewish laws, but on this occasion they broke many of their own rules. For example, criminal trials were supposed to be held during the day, not at night. To bear false witness was punishable by death, yet this group was actively looking for false witnesses. Evidence was to be corroborated by two witnesses, examined separately. And so we could go on. The trial was illegal.

No, this trial was not about exercising justice; this was about the authorities wanting rid of Jesus. The very people who knew their Scriptures in the Old Testament were not prepared to look openly at the evidence that God had sent the long-promised Messiah – Jesus.

Frustrated with the mess created by witnesses whose testimonies did not agree, Caiaphas asks Jesus the crucial question (v 63). Jesus breaks his silence and his answer is essentially 'yes'. He quotes from Daniel 7:13 (read v 14 too). That is all the chief priest needs and with his cry of 'Blasphemy!' chaos breaks out as Jesus is attacked, mocked and ridiculed.

Respond
God is passionate about justice. Pray for situations where justice needs to 'roll on like a river' (Amos 5:24).

Bible in a Year
Deuteronomy 19,20; Romans 4

Psalm 24

Sunday 25 March

Fling wide the gates!

Prepare
If you can, listen to Psalm 24 as a song, or sing a version you know.

Read
Psalm 24

Explore
On this Palm Sunday we are remembering and celebrating Jesus riding into Jerusalem, the Holy City, as King. He rides on a donkey and thus fulfils Zechariah's prophecy (Zechariah 9:9). On this occasion the crowds welcome him with words from Psalm 118:25,26 (all recorded in Matthew 21:1–11). As we have been reading over these last few days, the jubilation will soon change to hatred and loathing, such is the fickleness of humans.

In today's psalm David is declaring that God is King over all the earth and everything in it. He then ponders the question: who can enter into this holy God's presence? Only those who are holy, like him. Notice the emphasis on cleanliness and purity. Does anyone qualify? I certainly do not.

Then comes the call for the doors of God's dwelling place to open up (vs 7–10). Is this so that God can come out? No, it is so that the King of Glory can go in! Because Jesus entered Jerusalem as King many years later and went to his death on the cross, he is the one who ensures we can enter God's presence. Jesus is the King with clean hands and a pure heart. He is our forerunner, going ahead of us and making our acceptance by our heavenly Father possible.

> *Lift up your heads, you gates; be lifted up, you ancient doors, that the King of glory may come in.*
> Psalm 24:7 (NIV)

Respond
Bow down and worship, this is your King.

Bible in a Year
Deuteronomy 21,22; Psalm 35

Monday 26 March

Matthew 26:69–75

When courage fails

> Then he began to call down curses, and he swore to them, 'I don't know the man!' Immediately a cock crowed.
>
> Matthew 26:74 (NIV)

Prepare
Recall a time when your courage has failed and you have badly let down someone you love.

Read
Matthew 26:69–75

Explore
It had already been a very bad night and for Peter it was just about to get worse. At the point of Jesus' arrest all the disciples desert Jesus and run away (v 56). Then, only one of them, Peter, follows Jesus and the soldiers to the high priest's house. What do you think gave Peter the courage to follow at a distance and to linger to see what happened to Jesus?

Surely love for Jesus allowed Peter to overcome his fear and enter into enemy territory. Peter is experiencing what John would later describe in one of his letters: 'There is no fear in love' (1 John 4:18). Even when Peter is recognised, he does not leave immediately. Perhaps he is remembering, somewhere in his subconscious, what Jesus has taught about his followers acknowledging him in public (Matthew 10:32).

Peter is torn. Love for Jesus made him want to stay close, fear made him want to run for his life and led him to lie. It isn't until the third time he is challenged and he hears the cock crow that fear and shame overwhelm him and he leaves, distraught.

Peter's internal battle is one that is common to us all. Love for Jesus will always be at odds with love for ourselves.

Respond
Ask God's forgiveness for those times when love of self has triumphed over love for Jesus.

Bible in a Year
Deuteronomy 23,24; Romans 5

Matthew 27:1–10

Tuesday 27 March

Utter despair

Prepare
What is your strategy for moving forward when you know you have sinned?

Read
Matthew 27:1–10

Explore
Only God knows what motivated Judas to betray Jesus. There has been much speculation about it over the years. Was it greed? He does seem to have had a preoccupation with money (John 12:6). Did he end up hating Jesus because he was disillusioned with the way Jesus was bringing about revolution (26:55)? Perhaps he never intended that Jesus should die, but rather simply wanted to hasten Jesus achieving his mission: he wanted to prompt Jesus to act.

Whatever the motive for the betrayal, Judas clearly found it difficult to accept Jesus as he was. Judas thought he knew better and took things into his own hands. This is not uncommon in any of us. We find it difficult to accept Jesus and his ways and therefore go our own way. We take things into our own hands.

Notice what Judas does when he realises his guilt. He tries to put things right. But what is done is done and cannot be undone. His utter despair leads him to take his own life. If only he had been able to do the one thing that any of us can do when we recognise our guilt – turn to Jesus and seek his forgiveness. Consider how the chief priests show less sensitivity than Judas over an innocent man condemned to die.

> 'I have sinned,' he said, 'for I have betrayed innocent blood.'
> 'What is that to us?' they replied. 'That's your responsibility.'
> Matthew 27:4 (NIV)

Respond
Ask the Lord to help you run to him quickly when you know you have sinned.

Bible in a Year
Deuteronomy 25,26; Romans 6

Wednesday 28 March

Matthew 27:11–26

Crowd pleaser

> 'What shall I do, then, with Jesus who is called the Messiah?' Pilate asked.
> They all answered, 'Crucify him!'
> Matthew 27:22 (NIV)

Prepare
Call to mind some examples of corrupt governments in the world; actions of weak politicians and the consequences of bad leadership.

Read
Matthew 27:11–26

Explore
Go through the passage carefully and imagine you are an objective bystander. What do you see? What do you hear? What do you perceive? What impact does Jesus' silence have on the proceedings? Does this seem like a good way to reach a fair judgement?

In the early morning meeting (vs 1,2) the charge against Jesus has been changed. Pilate would not be impressed by a charge of blasphemy – he has no respect for Jewish laws and customs. So, a charge of treason has been cooked up (Luke 23:1,2). Pilate sees through the chief priests' ploy. He recognises that Jesus is an innocent man. Even his wife warns him against condemning him.

Pilate sees a possible way out by giving the crowd a choice of who should be released on this feast day. If he had been a stronger, more principled leader, would he have stood by what he knew of Jesus' innocence? Fear of the crowd and political expediency won the day. Washing his hands was not going to relieve him of responsibility (v 24). Being responsible for our actions is one of the features that marks us out as human. It is part of our dignity.

And so Barabbas, the guilty one, goes free and Jesus, the innocent one, is condemned to death. This is the gospel!

Respond
Pray for those in authority.

Bible in a Year
Deuteronomy 27,28; Romans 7

Matthew 27:27–44

Thursday 29 March

Mockery and derision

Prepare
Still your heart and mind and prepare to read a horrifying account of 'man's inhumanity to man' (Robert Burns, 1784).

Read
Matthew 27:27–44

Explore
We live in a violent and cruel world. We read in horror the way the Roman soldiers treat Jesus immediately prior to his crucifixion. Try not to skim over the bullying mockery, the taunting insults and the revolting spitting and hitting that Jesus endured. The only moment of grace in the midst of this horror is when Simon, from North Africa, is ordered to carry Jesus' cross-beam.

Through his trial and now through his mistreatment we see Jesus living out his own teaching. Glance through the Sermon on the Mount in Matthew 5–7 and notice 'But I tell you, do not resist an evil person … turn to them the other cheek … love your enemies.'

Walter Wangerin (*Reliving the Passion*, 1992) helpfully asks the question 'What has Jesus been doing since Gethsemane?' In these dark, seemingly endless, hours Jesus has been drinking the cup of suffering that the Father would not take away from him. Not just taking the mocking insults, but taking on the whole weight of human sin and shame.

The sad irony is that the very insults hurled at him were a twist on truth: he saved others precisely because he didn't save himself.

After they had mocked him, they took off the robe and put his own clothes on him. Then they led him away to crucify him.
Matthew 27:31 (NIV)

Respond
Read Isaiah 53 and worship your suffering Saviour.

Bible in a Year
Deuteronomy 29,30; Psalm 36

Friday
30 March

Matthew 27:45–56

Death and cosmic drama

> And when Jesus had cried out again in a loud voice, he gave up his spirit.
> Matthew 27:50 (NIV)

Prepare
Ponder this prophecy declared by Amos: '"In that day," declares the Sovereign Lord, "I will make the sun go down at noon and darken the earth in broad daylight"' (Amos 8:9).

Read Matthew 27:45–56

Explore

There is deep mystery here as we witness the Son of God dying on the cross. During the agonising six hours he cries out twice. His first utterance (v 46) is one of complete aloneness and despair: 'God made him who had no sin to be sin for us' (2 Corinthians 5:21). Sin inevitably brings separation from God. Jesus was going to a place unimaginably dark and evil so that you and I do not need to go there.

Jesus' second utterance was another loud shout. John tells he cried: 'It is finished' (John 19:30). In contrast to the first shout this has the mark of victory about it. The task is complete! At this point, in the midst of the agony of crucifixion, Jesus is still in control and willingly dies (v 50; see also John 10:18).

What do you make of the dramatic events that took place in the three hours from noon? The death of Jesus was of cosmic significance and there were some dramatic events around it. Nature reacts in the darkness and earthquake. What is being accomplished is shown in the Temple curtain tearing and in dead people rising – the way to God is opened and death is now a door.

Respond
Sit in amazed silence – this is our God.

Bible in a Year
Deuteronomy 31,32; Romans 8

Matthew 27:57–66

Saturday 31 March

Silent Saturday

Prepare

Have there been times when you have had to wait and watch, lost in the sadness and gloom of grief? It can seem as if the sorrow will never end.

Read

Matthew 27:57–66

Explore

Apparently not all members of the Jewish high council were supportive of Jesus being condemned to death (Mark 15:43). At least one of them had become his follower. Joseph now provides the tomb and prepares Jesus for burial.

Members of the Jewish authorities remember what Jesus' disciples seem to have forgotten (v 63). They break all their Sabbath laws and go to see Pilate again. They want this body guarded. Pilate agrees and sends soldiers. Every human effort is made to ensure that Jesus' corpse stays put (v 65)! Little would they have imagined what would actually happen. No one can shut what God has opened (Revelation 3:8).

All through this tragic, cosmic event, there are faithful witnesses; those who have not run away; those who have stayed with him, watching and waiting. Women who loved Jesus and followed him in life have followed to witness his death (vs 55,56,61). Imagine the depth of their sorrow as they stand in the shadows, unable to do anything, feeling helpless and abandoned. How will they live without this one they have come to love so deeply? All their hope has been placed in him. Now he lies dead and buried. Their world has fallen apart.

> *Mary Magdalene and the other Mary were sitting there opposite the tomb.*
> Matthew 27:61 (NIV)

Respond

'Lord, help me to hold on to you through the darkness I experience.'

Bible in a Year
Deuteronomy 33,34; Romans 9

Scripture Union

IT'S YOUR MOVE

A Young Person's Guide To Moving To **Secondary School**

Do you know a young person about to move to secondary school?

They've probably got questions going round in their head like:

- Will anyone like me?
- How am I going to get there?
- What will the lessons and teachers be like?

If so, this is the right book for them!

It's Your Move is a fun and friendly guide to moving to secondary school. Inside you'll discover lots of advice, together with stories of real people who have already made the move!

This is a great resource for churches to use to build relationships with local schools.

It's Your Move single edition
ISBN 978 1 84427 887 9
Price £3.50

It's Your Move pack (10 copies)
ISBN 978 1 84427 888 6
Price £20.00

ALSO AVAILABLE

IT'S YOUR CHURCH

Order from your local Christian bookshop | Order from Scripture Union: 01908 856006 | Order online www.scriptureunion.org.u